1972

The Story of Social Anthropology

Also by I. C. Jarvie

CONCEPTS AND SOCIETY

HONG KONG: A SOCIETY IN TRANSITION

MOVIES AND SOCIETY

REVOLUTION IN ANTHROPOLOGY

THE HISTORY OF SCIENCE

PREPARED UNDER THE GENERAL EDITORSHIP OF

DANIEL A. GREENBERG

THE
Story of Social
Anthropology

The Quest to
Understand Human Society

by I. C. JARVIE

McGraw-Hill Book Company

NEW YORK   ST. LOUIS   SAN FRANCISCO

DÜSSELDORF   LONDON   MEXICO

SYDNEY   TORONTO

DESIGN: HERB JOHNSON
ART DIRECTOR: HARRIS LEWINE

FIRST EDITION

Jarvie, Ian C
   The story of social anthropology.

   (The History of science)
   Bibliography: p.
   1.   Anthropology.   2.   Sociology.   I.   Title.
HM107.J35   301.2   70-39151
ISBN 0-07-032267-8

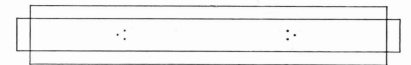

Contents

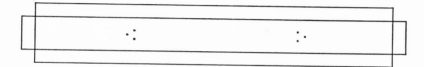

Introduction

DURING the late Pliocene period (from 14 million to 2 million years ago) some of the great variety of apes which inhabited East Africa probably left the forests and started roaming about on their hind legs in more open country. No longer needing their hands to hang from the branches of trees, they were free to use them to pick up sticks and stones. Their power to manipulate these was increased by the development of the thumb, and the outcome was the development of tools. The ape who uses tools is called man. Tools used intelligently were capable of making man the most powerful animal on earth. Tools used clumsily led nowhere. Thus men endowed with large and powerful brains which enabled them to use tools intelligently survived better. Their brain capacity was inherited by their descendants. Tools controlled by a big brain enabled man to hunt, cultivate, prosper, and develop a sophisticated new tool called language, and with the help of language a still more sophisticated tool called civilization.

All surviving tool-using apes have language as part of their technology. Not all have gone further and developed written languages, cities, bureaucracies, and civilization. It is tempting to think that civilization is a product of better brains, but this is refuted by the fact that normal infants of any human group can master the complexities of writing and civilization if they are reared in them from an early age. Nevertheless, despite similar capacities, men's efforts to live and work together in society result in very different outcomes from continent to continent, and even within the same continent. Chinese society is very different from American society. Plains Indians such as the Dakota (Sioux) are very different from Eastern forest-dwellers such as the Iroquois. They are different in such things as language, dress, family organization, housing, and means of livelihood. Having no desire to farm, the Sioux, after the introduction of the horse, roamed the plains hunting buffalo and living in the tepee or wigwam. The Iroquois, on the other hand, settled in villages, living in rectangular houses with barrel-shaped roofs, and grew crops such as corn.

Each of the many different ways of life can be regarded as a sufficient aid to survival. But, while all societies have survival value, some are more successful than others. By most measures of success—wealth and power; health, stature, strength, and longevity of the individual; and rate of population growth —the highly industrialized societies are more successful than the underdeveloped ones. Where two different societies come into contact, one more developed than the other (such as the Ancient Chinese civilization confronting the waves of barbarian hordes, or the West in its exploration of the world) the more powerful civilization sweeps all before it. Where underdeveloped countries succeed in coping with infant mortality, poor diet, and disease, it is usually because they borrow the inventions and ideas of the highly developed countries. Disparities between developed and underdeveloped were as marked in the times of Ancient China and of Ancient Greece as they are today. This persistent experience has tempted those in the more fortunate society to develop decidedly unfortunate attitudes toward their less-advanced neighbors.

As is the way with those who rise above their fellows, civilized man developed attitudes of superiority to those who were less successful. Civilized man looked around him and saw he had better tools; a written, not just a spoken, language; sophisticated social institutions such as towns; wealth; and power. He was tempted to look down on those without these things.

Today anthropologists no longer take it for granted that our more successful societies are better in every respect than their coevals. We allow that Congo Pygmies or Australian aborigines may have happier and more stable societies than ours. They have little or no neuroses or crime; they are harmoniously adapted to their harsh surroundings of jungle or desert and are secure in the cycle of the seasons and their religious beliefs. But these conclusions are very recent and not so common as our older attitudes of superiority. Early anthropology drew no distinction between success and superiority, but set out to explain them together. Modern anthropology attacks the assumption that success is the same as superiority. The history of anthropology is the history of how attempts to explain the superiority of some men over others gave place to criticism of the whole assumption: that success equals superiority. This led to better and less biased mapping of such differences as there are, and to the explanation of these differences as *diversities*, not as inferiority-superiority relationships.

The strongest early expression of the idea that human social differences are explained by some being superior to others is in Plato's *Republic* (fourth century B.C.). Plato explains the superiority and inferiority of men by comparing their souls to metals. Some metals are precious and others base; God has ordained that some are superior, some inferior. While this theory was never widely adopted, it was not coherently opposed until the theory of evolution made itself felt in anthropology in the late nineteenth century. This was the theory that men differed because they had evolved or developed at a different rate. Those lucky enough to invent the best tools, writing, and cities were able to profit from those inventions and advance rapidly. Those without, could not. The theory of evolution was less repellent than the theory of innate superiority; at least it denied no man the *potential* of being on a par with his fellows, even if it did deny the *fact* of his being on a par. Yet it did lend itself to the continued adoption of attitudes of superiority. Only in this century has evolution been modified by a critical attitude which sees societies and cultures as different modes of adaptation to the human situation, none in any straight-forward sense superior to others. Countries claiming superiority on account of their having abolished slavery, emancipated women, universalized the franchise and literacy in many places, and invented and adopted democracy are really claiming credit for achievements that not only *belong* to mankind as a whole but need to be *made available* to mankind as a whole—because all mankind is quite capable of benefiting from them.

Anthropology, then, can be seen as the story of man's attempts to come to terms with himself: where he came from, what he is, and what he should be. He once thought himself better than animals and better than "inferior" men. Later he learned that he evolved from animals, and that "inferior" men were simply those who had adapted to their surroundings in a different way. It is comforting to think oneself superior; but it is better neither to think or act as though it were true. Man faces a hostile environment and his only resources are his fellow men. The story of anthropology is in part the story of man's slow realization of this brotherhood and its consequences for his understanding of his species.

The story of anthropology, then, is simple in outline, but involved and intriguing in its details. In this short account we shall concentrate on only three areas: religion, the family, and social control. After surveying what has happened to our thinking on these topics we shall end with some discussion of what man has learned about the nature of himself and of his social setting. Before beginning, however, we should indicate how to view "society" for purposes of this book.

The society we live in is an amalgam of received *institutions*, such as marriage and the United States Congress; received *ideas*, such as romantic love and political freedom and equality before the law; *traditions* which embody both these institutions and their supporting ideas, such as the traditions of respect for contracts (such as marriage) and respect for the law in general; and *rights and duties* which we claim and internalize, respectively, such as our claim to the rights of freedom of travel or of the press, and such as our duty to behave properly or to aid those in need. We have received these things as part of our heritage, part of the society in which we have been reared and will eventually have to operate ourselves when the older generation yields control. Some parts of our heritage fill us with pride, like our traditions of tolerance, our democratic political institutions, and our strivings to help those both at home and abroad less fortunate than ourselves. To these parts of our heritage we feel we can give sustenance and support. Other parts of our heritage fill us with shame: entrenched crime and corruption, traditions and ideology of hatred, such as against nonwhites, Roman Catholics, Jews, foreigners, or nonconformists. These parts of our heritage we will wish we had not inherited, and we may seek ways to see to it that we do not in turn pass them on to our children. We will often fail in this as generations before us have, but we will feel the effort was worthwhile, however small the progress.

Such a way of looking at society, as a powerful inheritance, some of which we can modify and reject, does not much resemble the picture of society that would have been painted in Ancient Greece by Plato, in Ancient China by Confucius, or in the Middle Ages by Saint Thomas Aquinas. Our ideas about our own society, what it is and how we stand in relation to it, like our society itself, are a mixture of the received and of our own innovations. This book is in part an attempt to tell the story of how our present way of looking at society has evolved.

The Story of Social Anthropology

CHAPTER ONE

Magic, Religion, and Science

IN all societies religious beliefs and ceremonies are among the things men hold most dear. People have died for their religions and presumably will continue to do so. Christianity, Islam, Buddhism, Judaism, all have had their martyrs. There is no more convincing proof of absolute conviction than readiness to die. Is it not strange, then, that men are prepared to die for such diverse religions? But are religions diverse? If there is only one true religion are not all the others superstition? Perhaps. Which of us, however, can single out the true religion from the others? This looks easy enough. We tend to believe *our* religion is the true one, the others mere superstitions. Jews thought this of Romans, Romans thought this of Christians, Christians thought this of Muslims, and so on. The detached way anthropologists now look at this is very different from the way they looked at it when travelers and missionaries were exploring an unknown and unmapped Asia, Africa, and America. Indeed the major discovery of early anthropology might be the discovery of differences, and especially deep-seated religious differences, between societies. These differences then presented a problem to be explained. Differences of dress and of family size did not involve beliefs people

3

claimed to be *true*. It was just the way things were done. But on the questions of who the gods are, what they do, and how to worship and please them, beliefs were very strong and permeated many aspects of life. Some people were prepared to die for their beliefs.

Imagine this situation: An explorer comes across a people with weird beliefs that they staunchly stand by. Believing their religion to be a false one, the explorer asks: Why are they imprisoned in error? Why do they stick to it even when I explain how wrong they are? Are they thickheaded? Can it be that neither of us is right, that no one knows the answer? This latter conclusion is a sophisticated one which was mooted but not accepted in the Greek world and which gained currency only in this century.

In order for man to suspect that no one knows the answer, man first had to notice that his neighbor differed from him in important matters. Differences once discovered need to be explored. Extended explorations of other peoples' ways of life give one a fresh outlook when one turns back to look at one's own society.

Anthropology seeks to answer such questions as what is man, where did he come from, how does he fit into the scheme of nature? Two pairs of competing views arise to answer these questions. One pair divides over whether man is unique in nature and not understandable as just a part of it (for example, he has a soul and God watches over his welfare), or simply a very complex outcome of natural laws and developments. The other pair divides over whether man himself is one single species physically and morally or rather a widely divergent creature as various as his physical differences, as unequal as the different patterns of subordination and dominance suggest. Those who regard man as unique are likely to be suspicious of ideas that suggest man gradually evolved from other animals, such as apes. They will prefer ideas of an

4

act of creation, perhaps divine, which endowed man once and for all with his special features. Those who believe in the basic unity and similarity of man will be critical of theories showing man to be arranged in a hierarchy of race or intelligence or moral worth. By the twentieth century, all anthropologists saw man as part of nature and as one single species.

Since the fifteenth century is usually thought of as the Age of Discovery, it might be expected that anthropology could begin only after that. It serves no purpose to take a narrow view of the quest to understand man's differences. In the literature of Ancient Greece and Imperial Rome we find many descriptions of, and reflections on, the strange ways of alien and "barbarous" peoples. Compared with Ancient Egyptian depictions of the four races of mankind (over three thousand years ago) and Chinese descriptions of "barbarism," the range and depth of Greek discussions were great indeed. Before proceeding further, let us briefly mention some of these speculations, for most of the scholars who contributed to the history of anthropology in the seventeenth, eighteenth, and nineteenth centuries were themselves steeped in the classics.

How did man come to be? Throughout Greek thought two great ideas offer solutions to this. One is the myth of the Golden Age, a time in the distant past when man and society were in a state of golden perfection. Since that time the state of man had degenerated, and hope lay in a return to the Golden Age. The other is the idea of human progress: man is constantly improving his lot. By the fifth century B.C. progress had won a limited victory, and hope was in the future, not the past. The Greeks had developed the distinction between nature and convention, between what is and what should be. In the realm of nature the idea that man evolved from some other animal, probably aquatic, is found in Anaximander (611–547 B.C.). Empedocles (490–430 B.C.) was also evolutionist, and even developed a forerunner of Darwin's principle of natural selection, namely, that some changes in animals are poor adaptations to their surroundings and so die out. Thus is there a natural selection in favor of well-adapted changes. A little later in Democritus (c. 460–c. 370 B.C.) some scholars think there is a clear attempt to give a gradual, accidental, accumulative account of the development of technology and possibly also of language, in opposition to the traditional Greek view which treated inventions as divine. He sees technology as what makes man's progress possible, not as a mere prelude to progress.

These sophisticated speculations come down to us in fragments and are rarely backed by evidence of carefully studied and described societies. It was a long time before such intelligent ideas affected reporting of other societies. Take two examples: Herodotus and Caesar. One of the earliest of prose works, and indeed the first Greek and European prose masterpiece, the *Histories* of the Greek Herodotus (possibly composed between 430 and 424 B.C.), gives some succinct points about the religion of the Persians:

> The erection of statues, temples, and altars is not an accepted practice amongst them, and anyone who does such a thing is considered a fool, because, presumably, the Persian religion is not anthropomorphic [giving human properties to a thing not human] like the Greek. Zeus, in their system, is the whole circle of the heavens, and they sacrifice to him from the tops of mountains. . . . As for ceremonial, when they offer sacrifices to the deities . . . they erect no altar and kindle no fire, the libation, the flute-music, the garlands, the sprinkled meat— all these things familiar to us [Greeks], they have no use for; but before a ceremony a man sticks a spray of leaves, usually myrtle leaves, into his headdress, takes his victim to some open place and invokes the deity to whom he wishes to sacrifice. The actual worshipper is not permitted to pray for any personal or private blessing, but only for the king and for the general good of the community, of which he himself is a part. When he has cut up the animal and cooked it, he makes a little heap

6

of the softest green-stuff he can find, preferably clover, and lays all the meat upon it. This done, a Magus (a member of this caste is always present at sacrifices) utters an incantation over it in a form of words which is supposed to recount the Birth of the Gods. Then after a short interval the worshipper removes the flesh and does what he pleases with it. (*de Selincourt translation*)

This sort of heightened traveler's observation, where sympathy and understanding permeate the account, is, then, as old as European literature. There are many more examples in antiquity, including the works of the Roman historian Tacitus. Instead of those, I shall quote only a little from a much more famous Roman who made no pretense of being a professional scholar: Julius Caesar. In his *Conquest of Gaul* (about 51 B.C.) he writes of the customs of the Gauls:

As a nation the Gauls are extremely superstitious; and so persons suffering from serious diseases, as well as those who are exposed to the perils of battle, offer, or vow to offer, human sacrifices, for the performance of which they employ Druids. They believe that the only way of saving a man's life is to propitiate the god's wrath by rendering another life in its place, and they have regular state sacrifices of the same kind. Some tribes have colossal images made of wickerwork, the limbs of which they fill with living men; they are then set on fire, and the victims burnt to death. They think that the gods prefer the execution of men taken in the act of theft or brigandage, or guilty of some offence; but when they run short of criminals, they do not hesitate to make up with innocent men.

The god they reverence most is Mercury. They have very many images of him, and regard him as the inventor of all arts, the god who directs men upon their journeys, and their most powerful helper in trading and getting money. Next to him they reverence Apollo, Mars, Jupiter, and Minerva, about whom they have much the same ideas as other nations. . . . (*Handford translation*)

7

Sophisticated though Herodotus and Caesar were, their observations fall far short of the attempts to explain and understand other people's ways of life which is the core of anthropology as we now understand it. They make little attempt to show how the religions of the Persians and the Gauls fit in with their whole way of life. Instead they pick out a few curious or prominent features and leave it at that. Before observers could learn to treat societies as an interconnected working system, a great deal of anthropological argument had to be gone through. That argument is the history of anthropology.

One thing we have learned from the study of other societies is that we know our own society far less well than we think. In fact, anthropologists now explore and make "discoveries" in their own society. This last remark may seem a little odd; after all, we *live* in our own society, so we must surely be completely familiar with it. Perhaps so. But we are certainly not familiar with *all* aspects of the society in which we live. Our society is very large and complex and we have only a limited lifetime in which to move around and explore it. Moreover, some of its byways are quite closed to most of us. Few of us have explored the lives of the very rich, or of the extremely poor; in general we know little outside the boundaries of our immediate experience, and in a large society like the United States that outside is a huge area. Easterners know little of California; whites know very little about blacks. And of course sharp barriers are created by religion: few Protestants know what goes on among Catholics, just as few Christians know what goes on among Jews and vice versa.

Living in our own society, then, does not mean that we are familiar with all of it. There is always much to be explored and explained. We can "discover" things with which we are totally familiar, which are right under our noses, and we can explore them in ways which finally make us come to look upon them as very strange. Such things as our use of the words

8

cousin and uncle and aunt, so familiar to us, can come to seem almost inexplicable after years of study (see Chapter 2). Other customs, like that which forbids women to engage in manual labor and expects men always to behave deferentially toward them, are hard to understand when we come back to them with the enriched experience of having looked closely at other societies and social customs. Even now, it is hard to find much explanation of why our table manners are as they are, why we dress and cut our hair as we do, and so on.

Let us look a little more closely at some apparently familiar examples of religious behavior in our society. When boys and men go into a Christian church they are expected to remove their hats. Probably most people have never wondered why this is done, although if you asked them, they would doubtless say it was a sign of respect, such as the way men stand up when a lady comes into a room. (This raises other interesting questions: why do the particular gestures of remaining seated or keeping on one's hat indicate disrespect? Whereas in our society burping is rude, in many societies of the Pacific not burping after a meal is rude, indicating the meal was not pleasing.) But then, why are women, when they enter a Roman Catholic church, expected to wear a hat—or at least cover their heads in some way? It is not so easy to explain this gesture or to explain why women's actions are different from men's in this matter. A priest might say that in covering their heads women are also expressing respect, but that they *happen* to do it with a different gesture. And if asked why men and women do not show their respect in the same manner, the priest might give an answer like this. In the past women, especially married ones, showed their respect for men by covering their faces in public. They were the property of their husbands, and their features were not for other men to see. Slowly this gesture of covering the face took on overtones of respect, even of modesty. Obviously, in the presence of God in Church women wish to be both respectful and modest; thus,

in addition to being soberly dressed, they cover their heads—
a relic of the covering of the face practiced in ancient times.
Covering the face no longer has overtones of modesty; but
covering the head retains the character of a respectful gesture.

This explanation says that women's gesture of covering
their heads in Church has come by chance to signify respect,
and this gesture is observed by those wishing to signify respect.
The respect could have been shown in any number of other
gestures; it just so happens that our society has come to settle
on this one. (Cf. I Corinthians, 11:2–7.)

Whether or not this explanation satisfies, the reader may
wonder why gestures of respect are required at all. Why, for
example, do men show respect to women? To their elders?
We might show respect to older and more powerful people
and wish to please and placate them to ensure that they will
treat us well, not badly. Similarly men, who are nominally
more powerful than women, must please and placate women
when, for example, they want to get married. What is behind
our gestures of respect to God? Do we fear him and want to
curry his favor? Or is it more of a wooing relationship, like
that of men to women? In the Jewish and Christian traditions
God is conceived of as father and creator of us all, omniscient
and omnipotent. Sometimes he is even thought of as wrathful.
It is his power and his greatness that people wish to defer to.
Because our God is seen as a father and creator, we defer to
his presence when we enter church; some genuflect, some
bow, some kneel in prayer, some even close their eyes (although this may be for concentration rather than humility).

Is our way of behaving toward our god typical of the way
people in other societies behave? It is at this stage that the
question becomes strongly anthropological. One of the main
things anthropology does is to discuss problems which arise
in the course of comparing one society with another. Most
of us, however, do not visit other societies, especially very
strange ones, and even when we do it is rare that we stay long

enough to get to know them really well. The majority of us manage only brief stopovers in the course of journeys elsewhere. We are tourists, not anthropologists. Thus we are almost never in a position to make more than the most superficial of comparisons between our society and others. For this reason anthropology books are full of detailed stories about life in other societies—to help us to get to know them reasonably well without having to go there. If we were to observe an Islamic ceremony, we would notice that there are no women in the mosques at all, that there is no one who could be called the priest, and that the men wear their headgear and leave their shoes at the door. In Hong Kong or Singapore on the other hand, where Chinese people still worship their ancestors, we would be surprised by how casual the atmosphere in the temples is. People wander in and out; children play noisily nearby; no special clothes are put on or taken off; and sometimes there will be farm machinery present or even domestic animals roaming around. Yet when addressing the altar the worshipper bows deeply three times with his hands together, and speaks in a humble and stylized manner.

Different religions, then, demand different gestures of respect. But showing respect in some form seems to be universal, regardless of the particular gestures. Even in our own society we can observe wide differences in the manner in which this respect is shown. Whereas Christian men must take off their hats on entering church, Jewish men must cover their heads; whereas men and women worship together in Christian churches, in many synagogues the women watch the proceedings from a balcony and play a relatively minor role or none at all.

How do we explain this almost universal attitude of respect that men show to their gods? Anthropology is not just the demonstration by example that this respect *is* universal; it is also the attempt to explain the fact of this respect, and its universality: people everywhere respect their gods and express this in different ways depending on the customs and *mores* of their society.

Although this explanation seems obvious today, it was by no means obvious in previous ages. Christianity was predominant in our Western culture for over one thousand years. For most of that time we were hardly placed in a strategic position to see other religions in this tolerant light. Christianity, after all, claims to be the *only* true religion, Jehovah/Christ the *only* true God, salvation the *only* hope for any man's salvation. Christianity claims to be universal: the only correct religion for *all* men at *all* times. (At least, those men born late enough to hear Christ's teachings—the state of souls of people born before Christ lived is a moot point.) One measure of how Christianity is taken for granted by us is precisely the necessity of explaining these points in a book like this. Not all religions deny all others; not all gods slander and denigrate all others; not all religions consider it their sacred duty to make converts, to send out missionaries. A religion which does make all these claims is called "universalist." It can be contrasted with "tribal" religions: those which claim jurisdiction only over a particular social or cultural group and which tolerate neighbors with different gods. The Crusades, one of the great episodes of European history, were the result of the clash of two competing universal religions. Christian knights of Europe set out for the Holy Land to resist the armies of militant Islam. (Judaism is both universalist and tribal. Yahweh is both the God of Israel and the only God. Judaism does not do missionary work, but it does accept converts.)

At no time during this period of the dominance of Christianity can it be said that Westerners were aware of only one religion. But a lot of the time our civilization was quite ignorant of what actually went on in other times and other places. The Christian religion began, after all, as a small Jewish sect within the Palestinian provinces of the Roman Empire. It seemed to present no challenge to the sophisticated and tolerant Roman system of gods, although in the New Testament itself there are echos of a certain perturbation caused by the universalist claims of Jesus. (Notice how we are tempted by our Christian culture to add the word "pagan" to our description of Roman religion. The word suggests the "heathen"—neither Christian, Jew, nor Muslim—or the "unenlightened.") Then, after a time, Christianity spread as far as Rome and, finally, by the conversion of the Emperor Constantine in the fourth century, it became the religion of Roman Europe. But it would be a mistake to assume that from then on it ruled unchallenged: we have only to read the lives of the church fathers and about the trials for witchcraft in the Middle Ages to realize that Christianity was far from passing unchallenged. Various features of our Christmas festival show traces of the religion Christianity replaced. There are the relics of Yuletide, such as mistletoe and the log. There is the fact that Christmas is celebrated by feasting as was the primitive midwinter festival. Once the year turned, thoughts turned toward spring and renewal. Christmas coincides with the midwinter solstice in the Julian calendar, regardless of there being no date of birth for Christ mentioned in the Bible, although there is an ancient Eastern tradition that the birth was on January 6. The eminent anthropologist Sir James Frazer argues that Jesus' birthday was not celebrated by the early church for this very reason.[1] All this shows us that Christianity took over for one of its festivals a pre-Christian festival day along with some of its associations and traditions.

At its inception, Christianity adapted itself to local conditions. However, by the time of the age of the voyages of discovery and exploration of the world, Christianity had had almost monolithic sway over Europe for one thousand years. It therefore came as a shock when travelers and explorers told of bizarre practices among "savages" which appeared to con-

---

[1] Sir James Frazer, *The Golden Bough*, abridged edition, Macmillan (St. Martin's Library), London, 1957, chap. 37.

13

stitute their "religions." Reports of ceremonies that included dancing, magical gestures, belief in spirits, ritual murder and sacrifice, weird sexual practices, and other oddities struck people as so unlike Christianity, the model for what religion should be, that they were labeled the irrational delusions of the childlike minds of savages. This amounted to a theory to explain savage religion—to explain why it was so unlike Christianity or the other world religions. For long, indeed, there was serious dispute about whether these "savage" practices could be classified with what came to be called the "higher" religions at all. Were they not the crudest superstition and mumbo jumbo, not worth the attention of civilized men?

Both theories—that savages had no religion, or that such as they had was mere childish delusion—had one major consequence. The value Western explorers placed on savage religions was low, and it was felt that mankind (and savages) could not but benefit if these practices were extinguished and replaced by Christianity; and where the savages could not be converted, the worst excesses of their barbarism could be curbed by superior force. This combination of the self-confident idea that Christianity is a religion for all peoples, to be introduced or imposed in all situations, and the superior conviction that what savages believed was not to be taken seriously or highly valued, was a devastating one. It justified colonialism and missionary work, bribery, and even force. It is not too strong to say that havoc was wreaked on many primitive societies by missionary activity, despite the fact that that activity was often engaged in with the best of motives, and by the most serious and thoughtful of men.

When people set out to discover why there were such differences of religion, they were practicing anthropology. The feeling that any religion which did not resemble Christianity needed explanation is obvious, given three things: (1) the universalist claims of Christianity, (2) the scant information that was available about other world or great religions, and (3) the theory of natural religion. The problem for the universalist is: why is the rest of the world unenlightened? The answer is because God chose to reveal himself only at a particular point in time and space, relying on the light of truth to illuminate and spread through the darkness. However, there were many layers of darkness and of error and of savagery to be penetrated before that light could shine. This explained why the gospel did not always have such an easy passage in its spread.

The other great world religions, Judaism, Buddhism, and Islam, were a complicated problem. Despite deep enmity toward them and a conviction of their error, Christians felt able to understand and appreciate them to some extent. While the religion of barbarians was anathema, the rival claims of the world religions, like those of Christian heretics, were more a matter of error, to be solved by prayer and reasoning and, only in extreme cases, violence. For example, all these rival world religions were monotheistic; they had many moral prohibitions in common with Christianity; they were clearly the work of civilized and thoughtful people who commanded a written language; and they were themselves based on sacred scriptures. How different seemed the religions of savages! How sunk in moral turpitude, how inhuman, how intellectually wayward! Today it is difficult to understand sympathetically this anthropological snobbery; it is very remote from our emotional center, and so are the problems to which it gave rise. But as we are stressing all along in this book, our present state of thinking on these matters has come about only because of what has been thought out and argued out by previous generations.

The third factor mentioned is natural religion. This is not a religion itself, but a theory about the origins of religion. It was developed in opposition to the idea that religion has been revealed: an individual act of conversion or revelation was necessary for a person to become religious. The theory of natural religion claimed that God was in evidence in nature and creation and that perfectly reasonable arguments and ideas indicated his existence and character. Thus religion was a phenomenon any man could acknowledge, without revelation. The complication is that this theory is democratic: it assumes that religion is accessible to all men unaided by revelation or by priests. But then the existence of savage (from the French *sauvage*, wild, natural) men immediately raises a difficulty. Why, if religion is natural, has not man living in the state of nature some such religious beliefs? The question is further complicated by conflicts of evidence. Some of the savages early discovered, especially in Polynesia, were serene and did have religious ideas not frightfully out of kilter with the ideas of natural theology (the test of this was often taken to be monotheism—if they had *that* they couldn't be too bad). But other primitive peoples, like the American Indians, and many African tribes, seemed to be far beyond the pale. They were not theists, they had cruel moral codes, they were superstitious about darkness, and so on. How were their beliefs to be explained? Either the theory of natural religion was false, or these savages were corrupted, degraded, or had in some other way been perverted from what is apparent to all reasonable men. This suggests still another explanation: They were not in the true sense completely reasonable men. They were a bit irrational, perhaps even a bit childish, and so what could be expected of them?

Before we go on, something has to be said about this idea that some savages had no religion. Anthropologists today have not reported a people anywhere in the world that is without religion. Why were our forebears so gullible about this? A number of factors were involved. Many reports about remote peoples were based on very short visits by observers far from detached. It takes a while to get to know the religious practices, or any practices, of a people. More important, the reporters rarely knew the local language and could not ask about what they did not see, or even about what they did see and did not understand. Finally, most savage societies did not have writing, and so, whatever their religions were, they did not have their basis in a text or sacred book. Thus poor observation, poor understanding, and the lack of literacy formed a barrier to the study of other people's religion.

The answers to the question of why some savages had no religion had a profound influence on Christians not so much because the reporters were misinformed but because no one realized they were misinformed.

Tension was being generated because two quite incompatible images of savages were being entertained simultaneously. The primary image seems to have been that savages are bloodthirsty, backward, pagan, cruel, irrational, totally unenlightened in their cloacal darkness. Hence all the overtones that the word "savage" carries, and hence too the opposition of contemporary anthropologists to using this word at all, since it still carries the overtones of denigration. Thomas Hobbes, writing about society and politics in the seventeenth century, pictured the life of man in a state of nature as "solitary, poor, nasty, brutish and short."[2] There can be little doubt that he was talking about the life of man in the raw and that what he conceived this state of nature to be had a lot to do with the descriptions of savage life which were circulating in the travel literature of his time. And yet, in Locke, writing a little later in the seventeenth century his famous *Treatises of Government,* we have quite another image presented to us: natural man beginning to see the need for rules to protect life and property. This new awareness led man to enter into an agreement or contract with his fellow men in order to formulate and ensure respect for these rules, thereby securing a tolerably peaceful life. By the eighteenth century the social reformer Rousseau presents us with a romantic vision of savage life—the "noble

2 Thomas Hobbes, *Leviathan,* 1651.

savage." This view is the complete reverse of Hobbes's picture. The noble savage is pure, upright, loving, honest, wise, and rather pantheistic.

It is difficult even today for us to decide what to think of primitive peoples. The Red Indian, for example, is sometimes portrayed in movies and on television as a bloodthirsty villain; other times he is a heroic figure struggling against the harshness and force of the white man. These various approaches are no different from the struggles of philosophers like Plato, Hobbes, and Locke in deciding on their view of man. We are better informed about the facts these days, but the facts always have to be interpreted. Everyone has to make up his own mind on anthropological issues, because the facts do not tell us how to judge people. Awareness of more facts, however, may save us from foolish interpretations. That Hollywood or television seems unable to decide whether to portray savage Indians as heroes or villains might lead us to ask why they should. Red Indians sometimes were heroic, sometimes were villainous. When we see white people in movies as villains and as heroes we do not conclude that Hollywood cannot make up its mind about white men. We *know* white men are diverse. We have to realize that so-called savages are diverse too.

Those in the seventeenth and eighteenth centuries who thought so highly of the noble savage, who saw him as embodying all the qualities of character and spirit, all the moral virtues they admired, had also to face the fact that the noble savage was not a Christian. This may have been dismaying, since virtue, character, and spirit were at that time attributed to strong religious faith. It was hardly possible to claim the noble savage as a "natural" Christian, since God is a personal god and the savage does not even know this name, still less his Son's life and teachings. This too sat uneasily with the theory of natural religion: if God had appeared in our culture, why not also to the savage? These questions had to be faced because Christianity made universalist claims; it claimed to be the religion of salvation for *all* men. The noble savage could really only be classified in two ways: either he had some natural religion, or he had none. If none, then perhaps he is not so noble after all. In other words, savages who were not Christians could be classified either as simple and good yet partially or wholly unenlightened; or they could be unenlightened because they were bad and corrupt. This forced a polarization between the Rousseauist position and its Hobbesian opposite extreme, and the tensions between these poles constantly discharge during anthropological discussions of the savage and his ways in the nineteenth century. Most of the time the "savage" savage was the predominant image of the nineteenth century; it is only in the present century that we get a wholehearted return to Rousseauism.

It is of interest to note that the imputation of childishness to savages reflects also on the current theories of what children are really like. In Victorian mythology they were little angels, pure and innocent. Yet constantly, it was felt, they had to be steered onto the straight and narrow path because they had no resistance to corrupting influences. Few regarded children as unholy little beasts to be consigned to the back stairs as much as possible. Yet the English preference for sending children away from home to boarding school has curious undertones. In this century, again, there has been a reversal. Freud, who was steeped in the writings of the anthropologist Frazer, toppled the pure-child theory by attributing motives of envy, hatred, and lust to innocent babes. Things have never been the same since. The novelist William Golding has made two interesting examinations of these anthropological themes. In *The Inheritors* he tries to envisage what life was like among the half-ape, half-men we might call the "missing link." In *Lord of the Flies* he shipwrecks some "pure and innocent" choirboys and watches their basic savagery and cunning rise through the veneer of civilization as the struggle for survival takes over.

Into the somewhat fruitless conflict between savages conceived as unenlightened good and savages conceived as unenlightened bad came a quite new anthropological idea from the theory of evolution: savages were not unenlightened but *earlier*. Charles Darwin and Alfred Wallace in 1858 crystallized for biology the theory of evolution. This theory, which has origins in ancient Greek thought and was very much in keeping with the intellectual atmosphere of the midnineteenth century, suggested that the proliferation of animal and plant species on earth was to be explained by saying that some had evolved from others. This notion of evolution—gradual change—suggested an explanation of the close similarity of animal families to one another. Could it be that one had changed into another? Could it be that single-celled animals had bred multicelled, that fish had bred lizards, that apes had bred man? Over huge ranges of time by gradual changes this seemed plausible. Doubtless some creatures, like the dinosaurs, were viable at certain times, but could not survive radical changes in their surroundings. The ingenious camouflage of plants, insects, birds, and other animals suggested that living creatures are very sensitive to their surroundings; they adapt to them. The ability of a new species to adapt decides whether it will survive. If it cannot stand the climate, eat the food available, or cannot escape its enemies, it will disappear.

Hitherto the many species had been looked upon as God's handiwork of creation in all its variety. But Darwin noted that similar plants and animals differed in many small ways that had less to do with beauty than with the environment they inhabited. This led him to argue that over many years plants and animals adapt themselves to the conditions in which they live; for example, their coloring may give them better camouflage, their bodies may change to allow them to hunt food better or escape more easily. How could all this purposive adaptation be brought about if not by God's genius?

Because, Darwin argued, those species which were better adapted survived to breed new generations; those poorly adapted died out. This selection in favor of the fittest he called "natural selection."

There was religious opposition to Darwin from the beginning, since his ideas contradicted the Biblical story of creation, left little place for God or miracles, and undermined the idea that all creatures have a unique and divinely given "nature" which makes them what they are. Aside from these direct quarrels over the truth of evolution, the theory, if accepted, helped to explain primitive religions.

Evolution suggested that savage beliefs were at an earlier stage of development on the road to higher religions (as they came to be called), just in the same way as the amoeba is at an earlier stage than fish, fish at an earlier stage than apes, and apes at an earlier stage than man. (There were certain misconceptions about evolution here which we shall mention later.) Thus neither ignorance, stupidity, childishness, nor badness were needed to explain the unsatisfactory nature of primitive religion. Now, on the contrary, a great new field for thought was opened up. Assuming, as our forebears quite naturally tended to do, that their own civilization was the best and most enlightened ever to grace the face of the earth, the question became, how did its components develop? In religion this became: trace back the evolution of the idea of God becoming man; trace back the evolution of the idea of the trinity; trace back the evolution of the use of music and singing in worship and so on. It was immediately and uncritically assumed that this tracing could be done among primitive peoples, because they were clearly at earlier stages through which we ourselves probably passed. Primitive peoples were "living fossils" or our "living ancestors."

In this way evolution also affected missionary attitudes. Considering that savages were now seen as simply at an earlier stage of development, it became a new sacred duty for missionaries to go and help bring "our backward brothers" up to our level of understanding of the world. Thus not only religion but education needed to be spread, and this task was undertaken enthusiastically by the churches. Setbacks and resistance to missionaries among native peoples could now be understood and taken less to heart since the process of education must obviously be gradual, like evolution itself.

The idea that religion, like other things, has evolved from simpler beginnings was a very powerful one. Even today, it remains the standard view of most people uninitiated into the social sciences. Evolution explained so much so easily that it was a remarkably useful tool. No one, however, had yet explained how religion really fits into the evolutionary theory of the survival of the *fittest*. What constitutes a "fit" religion? What is a "fit" religion fit for? Indeed, when it comes to mapping in the details of this idea of religious evolution, answers to these questions are hard to find. It is easier to describe what would *not* be fit. An unfit religion would be one that destroyed the society. It is possible to say simply that the measure of the adaptive efficiency of a religion is the survival of the society itself. A religion which actively and success-fully encouraged suicide of the individual could wipe out a society. A society that wipes itself out is hardly adapted to survive. Other forms of self-destroying religion would be those which absolutely prohibited sexual congress, or made castration compulsory, or forbade the slaughter of man-eating beasts. There is a legend about a tribe in India that held all life to be sacred and forbade all taking of life, including that of the plentiful man-eating tigers of the locality. This tribe did not last long. So at the very least a religion must not destroy the society it belongs to. But we are still in need of an explanation of all the many different kinds of religion which are compatible with social survival.

An attempt to provide such an explanation is found in the most monumental anthropological work of the late nineteenth century, *The Golden Bough.* In this work, the great scholar Sir James Frazer amassed twelve volumes of material from all over the world on human sacrifice, priest-kings, the worship of trees, and so on. (Frazer also took a certain pleasure in drawing parallels between the rituals of primitive peoples and those of Christianity, for here were very backward people with religious beliefs uncomfortably like those of Western Europe. One conclusion from this would be that religion is a constant factor in the lives of all men; another would be that the survival of religion in Western Europe was a relic of our primitive past. At any rate, the smug conviction that European religion was unique and qualitatively superior to primitive religion was never again to be taken seriously.)

Even though Frazer's originality can be called into question (E. B. Tylor was a contemporary influence) and although not all of it is accurately reported and not all the sources are reliable, *The Golden Bough* is packed with extraordinary anecdotes and customs. Frazer sets out to trace all the roots and connections of a strange ritual in which a priest-king lived in constant fear of attack. Anyone who wished to succeed him had to slay him and take possession of the sacred tree from which power came. But the victor could never rest easy as sooner or later some challenger would try to sneak up on him, kill him in his turn, and take over. In collecting the vast amount of material for *The Golden Bough,* Frazer makes the attempt to fill in details of how religion evolved gradually. He does not try to explain all the different brands of religion, but concentrates only on the evolution of what he takes to be the three main subdivisions: magic; religion, which evolved from magic; and science, which evolved from religion.

In outline his theory is as follows. Magic, science, and religion are not completely different things; they are simply different ways of explaining what happens in the world. Each is a framework which allows one to explain events; they differ in their success at explanation and in their rationality. In the beginning there was magic. Primitive man, striving for explanation of his surroundings, and perhaps especially of disasters like disease and death and hunger, seems to have quite naturally come to believe the world was not haphazard but explicable. However, what happened was clearly not under his control; therefore it must be controlled by something else. What? Well, one idea which presented itself was control by a mysterious world of spirits—powerful, invisible, yet all-pervasive.

How could man come to think the visible, tangible things of this world were under the sway of entities as mysterious as spirits? Perhaps he was able to conceive of spirits because of the mysterious character of various familiar, everyday things. Air, for example, is invisible, present everywhere, vital to life (as breath) and permeable; yet, in the form of wind, or of breath condensing on cold days, it can be quite tangible. Breath has, indeed, often been associated with man's soul or spirit, his life: a newborn baby dies if it is not induced to breathe; at death a man "breathes his last." Death itself is mysterious. Where there was a person, there now lies a corpse —in all visible ways the same, but without life, without breath, without movement. Loss of life, breath, movement, has taken place invisibly, mysteriously. Where has this person's life gone?

Other commonplace things are hard to explain, too. A person's shadow follows him everywhere, except when there is no bright light. A person lies down to sleep and wakes up knowing he has remained in the same place; yet while asleep he has, as we say, dreamed of doing and seeing things in all sorts of places. Clearly his body stayed put—which part of him took part in the dream? The idea, then, that man has an intangible but important side to him can be seen to agree with common experience. So belief in spirits, ghosts, and other mysterious but powerful entities makes sense in the terms in which primitive man sees and understands the world. Just as primitive man swings his stone axe, so must the invisible spirits (resembling man in this way) hurl the thunderbolts, control the spread of terrifying things like droughts and plagues and famines.

In one view, this primitive kind of explanation of natural phenomena can be called animism because it suggests that there are animating (that is, life-giving) spirits guiding and controlling all objects and events, and because it denies that there is anything accidental, anything inanimate. Certainly this primitive kind of explanation is anthropomorphic: it attributes human or animal characteristics to nonhuman and nonanimal things. But the best general name for this sort of explanation of natural phenomena is "magic." Magic can come in many forms and subtypes. European magic, like the casting of spells, the brewing of potions, the sticking of pins into statuettes, the wicked congress with the devil incarnate, can be labeled "sorcery"; Greek magic, like that of the oracle at Delphi, which gave forth riddling but profound answers to problems, or African magic, which believes witches have a special organ in their bodies that makes them capable of bringing about evil events, can be called "witchcraft" and its practitioners "witches."

Whatever one calls it, it was Frazer's theory that magic was the most primitive explanation of events and things. Clearly he meant that it was also historically the earliest in the development of mankind. But it can also be regarded as logically the simplest answer, since it is based on a direct analogy with common human experience, our experience of initiating a series of events. When I want to move my car, I get into it, start it, and move it. Magic simply says that things happening around us are being initiated by invisible forces or beings or spirits. Cultures exist where all of daily life is guided by magic. In particular, the Australian aborigines were held up by Tylor and Frazer as obviously the most primitive of surviving peoples since they appeared to have only magic and nothing resembling religion. (This theory was a mistake; the aborigines do have a religion.)

Now how did primitive man get from the stage of magic to the stage of religion? Evolutionists tried to put themselves in the shoes of the primitives. How, they asked themselves, could we have moved from one to the other? Well, what does the move consist of? For one thing it consists of replacing the occult (supernatural) forces and spirits of magic with the specific idea of powerful, even all-powerful gods. For another thing it involves replacing the constancy of magic with the anthropomorphic features of gods, who cannot simply be manipulated but must be appeased, praised, supplicated and sacrificed to, and so on. On the basis of these features it seemed that the main change was from the regularity of the world conceived under magic to the rather erratic nature of the world as conceived by religion.

Why would magic ever give way to religion? Well, for one thing, magic does not work. Magicians say that if it does not work it is because the spell was not carried out properly, but that excuse will wear thin after a while. Magic does not fail all the time. Sometimes sick people will get better. *We* may think that recovery had nothing to do with spells; those who believe in magic will say it does. And so, if a method works sometimes and not others it might seem to be willful or even capricious, that is, not displaying any obvious pattern. Perhaps, in addition to the forces of magic, the world is inhabited by powerful creatures we have come to call gods. No spell will work with them; and appeals to gods, such as prayers, will be answered if they feel like it. Thus the world appeared capricious and thus religion was added to magic (most societies have both).

Again, religion is modeled on man's experience of himself. When we think of things as capricious, we can either conclude that the situation is one of anarchy, no order at all, or we can seek a model or pattern sufficiently complicated to match the

26

apparent disorder. To early man the model for caprice was himself; he conceived the idea that the universe is being controlled by beings or spirits very much like himself: these were gods. Like man, nature was capricious because she was controlled by capricious gods. In some cultures, like those of Ancient Greece and Ancient India, this analogy is very close. These cultures conceive of there being many gods, each with different dominant characteristics, some more powerful than others. Events can be explained by the capriciousness, lust, or mischievousness of these beings. However, unlike man, but like the forces of magic, these gods were invisible and immortal.

In the religions of the world we see a display of the many different attempts men have made to say what they think their gods are like. Some religions tolerate all the others. Their attitude is that "our tribe has its religion, your tribe has yours." In Africa, too, there is rarely religious competition. Other religions claim to be best by virtue of their being able to incorporate all others, for example, Taoism in China, or that of the Romans, who could simply add gods to their pantheon at will. Still other religions are universalist: they claim to be the sole possessors of religious truth and they crusade against others and also try to convert. Mohammed said: "There is no God but God and Mohammed is his prophet." This does not mean anything unless it is seen in the context of fierce religious competition. And unless one grasps this claim to exclusive possession of truth one cannot understand the Islamic Holy War against the infidels (excluding the Jews whom Mohammed called the "People of the Book") or the Christian Crusades against the Antichrist. (Less easy to understand is the claim of Judaism to be the one true religion of the one true God, while at the same time refusing to proselytize, that is, to recruit members, making it difficult for people to convert.)

The great anthropologists Tylor and Frazer, then, argued that religion was an attempt to explain what happens in the world by reference to a god or gods—mysterious and intangible beings, not unlike men in some ways, who are able to sway the destinies of the world. Both authors recognized that social evolution from one stage of development, such as magic, to another, such as religion, did not take place in a simple and straightforward way. Most societies, for example, still had magical practices even when they had also developed religion.

The aborigines of Australia, to take a concrete case, have religious cults surrounding a sky-hero, a mother goddess, a serpent, and various totemic objects and animals, the details varying from one part of the country to the other. Coexisting with these elaborate religions are belief in sorcery (the making of evil magic) and medicine men (magicians who cure). Knowing nothing of the theory that serious diseases are caused by germs, they believe that magical actions by other people or by spirits are the cause and must be neutralized by the medicine men.[3] The Mende, an agricultural people 700,000 strong living mainly off rice in the southwestern part of Sierra Leone and the adjoining part of Liberia, have a complex of traditional beliefs dominated by a notion of "God," a supreme being who created the earth and everything in it. There is also a cult around the dead ancestors. Grafted onto this traditional religion is Islam, and of course missionaries have converted some Mende to Christianity. All Mende turn to magic for protective charms, help with love affairs, or to further their careers. A good example of how a religion can merge into magic is the practice of writing a chapter of the Koran on a wooden board and washing off the Arabic characters with water, which is then bottled and serves to endow its possessor with a commanding personality.[4] Among the Indians of North America animistic religion and belief in magic were universal. Sometimes the books refer to the religious specialists as both

[3] A. P. Elkin, *The Australian Aborigines*, Doubleday, New York, 1964.
[4] K. Little, *The Mende of Sierra Leone*, Routledge and Kegan Paul, London, 1951.

shamans (magicians) and priests. The Creek Indians, formerly of Alabama and Georgia, to take an example, believed in a supreme deity who lived in the sky and was associated with the sun. They also had at least four kinds of medicine men: knowers who prophesied the future and diagnosed disease; healers; those who worked the weather, especially rain; and witches or wizards whose activities were often evil.[5]

These examples are taken from modern sources, but information of similar mixtures was known to Frazer and Tylor. But, believing magic to be decisively the more primitive notion, these anthropologists suggested that the relative amounts of magic and religion in a culture were good guides to the antiquity of the culture. The more magic, the older the culture; the more religion, the later the culture. (Their assumption that a culture cannot alter in several respects yet retain its magic is contentious and was challenged by later anthropologists.)

Similarly, as magic coexists with religion in some societies, so does religion with science. For some reason Frazer did not pay much attention to the fact that magic coexists with science, as in our own culture. A farmer in our society may select the best hybrid corn seed available (science), plant it under a waxing moon (magic), and even pray to God for rain when he goes to church on Sunday (religion). It seemed to Frazer logical enough that as a more sophisticated way of explaining the world became available, it would gradually oust the more primitive explanation. Thus at the climax of the whole scheme of development came the scientifically based civilization of Western Europe. It was still, of course, trimmed with religion; but that could be explained as something left over in the course of evolution, bound sooner or later to disappear.

But now the problem was to explain how man made the mental transition from religion to science, for this seems to be

[5] Harold E. Driver, *Indians of North America,* University of Chicago Press, Chicago, 1961.

a leap indeed. The answer is simple but surprising, because it leads to the discovery of a resemblance between magic and science that is scarcely believable at first sight. Religion views the events of the world as capricious: unpredictable, although not entirely indifferent to our pleas. Magic views the world as open to manipulation because it behaves in a regular and predictable manner, and if only one knows how—spells, potions, and so on—one can get what one wants. Religions allowed sacrifice, prayer, plea, good works, and so on, to influence the gods; but none of these was guaranteed to produce results. A distinguishing feature of religion, in fact, is that it does not promise that adequate worship procedures will result in the desired event coming to pass in this world. No one guarantees that your prayers will be answered; the gods in their wisdom may decide to deny you their favor. Some religions stave off the cashing of all checks for devotion and good behavior to the next world. (However, the sophisticated have been known to argue that worldly success is a sign of God's grace.) The Manus of the Admiralty Islands in the South Pacific have a religion which slightly complicates the picture. They have a form of ancestor worship in which the relic of the particular ancestor (usually his skill) can be abused and even thrown out and replaced if he proves unable to bring good fortune to his surviving family.

A further complication is the case of China, where religion proliferates in all directions, but only some of it is connected with direct rewards. The core of classical Chinese religion was the worship of Heaven (the supreme spiritual power of the universe) and its pantheon of subordinate deities, and the worship of ancestors. The ancient book *Li Chi* states, "All things stem from Heaven, and man originates from ancestors." This was a state religion conducted by officials and civic leaders. At the close of the second century A.D., in a period of social upheaval, Taoism, a religion which preached universal brotherhood, a return to simplicity and good works, arose.

A little later, with the turmoils and calamities continuing, Buddhism spread from India and Central Asia, at first in small ways, but soon it was a great Chinese religion, officially patronized. In one of its forms, Buddhism, like Taoism, fostered magic cults. Hinayana Buddhism emphasized the attainment of magical power to ward off demonic influences which wrought misery in the human world. Mahayana Buddhism, with its doctrine of pity for all creatures and salvation for all humanity as the only possible means of achieving personal salvation, lifted Buddhism above the level of individual rewards and magical techniques. Lesser gods were looked to for favor; different gods were prayed to for different purposes. House gods; ghosts and spirits; gods and goddesses of mercy, the sea, wealth; patrons of crafts and trades—all these and many more were mixed together in a way that varied from north to south, district to district, village to village, even individual to individual. And so Chinese religion sanctions those who display a selfless devotion to prayer and also those who make a direct appeal to an ancestor to help them pass an examination.

For Frazer and Tylor the key question is how the beliefs explain the events of this world. If the caprice of gods, ghosts, and spirits is used, then they can see a clear contrast with science. The invention of science means the restoration of order and regularity to the world, a rejecting of both religion and magic by insisting that what causes events to happen must be observable and concrete, not invisible and mysterious. This view is the heart of science, according to Tylor and Frazer; this is what separates the high Western civilizations from the backward magical-religious civilizations. Again they made a serious if understandable mistake. Science appeals to many strange and invisible entities like forces, atoms, chemical bonds, and so on, that by definition cannot be seen.

Take an example. If there is a person suffering from a serious disease, what should be done? If the society is dominated by magical ideas, the illness is attributed to someone casting an evil spell on the person and attempts are made to make a counterspell, perhaps even killing the witch responsible, if he can be discovered. In a society which is dominated by religious views, the disease may be attributed to any number of causes, but God or the gods are asked to intervene and help the sick person get well. Thus prayers are said. In a society whose ethos, that is, guiding belief, is scientific, the sickness is attributed either to some internal lack of balance in the body, or to its invasion by germs of some kind. After conducting tests to determine what specifically caused the illness, the doctors prescribe some substances (drugs) or procedures (perhaps surgery) which will help cure the disease. Whereas magic attributes disease to controllable forces and science attributes disease to general processes that can be understood, religion gives no clear account of disease and makes no promises about alleviating it. Science removes the capriciousness of religion and restores the regular, understandable picture of a world that obeys definite laws, such as the laws of physics, chemistry, biology, medicine, and so on.

We can see from this account how oversimplified anthropology was then. In our own society, for example, prayers and drugs coexist in hospitals. How can we tell if this mixing up of the neat categories is not true of remote societies? The answer is, to do research. But a remarkable feature of all the anthropologists we have mentioned is that they never went near the primitive tribes which existed in their day and age. They relied entirely on the published reports of travelers and missionaries and on correspondence with people in remote parts. But in the late nineteenth century in America, and gradually elsewhere, students of anthropology began to argue that it was essential to visit these societies in person, and to see for oneself what they were really like. In America, such a change of approach had a lot to do with the guilt felt over the Indian wars and led to the belief that the white man could learn a lot from those previously dismissed as savages. Be that as it may, expeditions to spend time with Indians and Africans and Orientals and Australian aboriginals gave us much information that did not fit into the pattern of magic-science-religion. The story of the anthropology of religion after Frazer is the story of criticism accumulating to the point where many of his ideas had to be discarded.

This idea that magic preceded religion and religion preceded science is, as we have seen, plausible; it is so plausible and simple that this idea is still widely diffused in the popular understanding of magic. But as research into magic and religion continued, it became clear that there was much more to be said. For one thing, it was difficult to check up on whether the evolutionary sequence of magic, religion, and science had really occurred. Indeed *all* reconstructions of the past history of mankind were difficult to check before the process of dating by computing rates of decay of radioactive substances was invented. Just because the logical structure of magic theories is simple, it does not prove that they are earlier. As we shall see, there are kinship systems such as those among the Australian aborigines (long popularly thought to be the "most primitive" peoples) which are much more complicated than our own. So primitivity and logical simplicity need not go together. For another, Frazer, especially, was inclined to say that magical thinking preceded religious thinking which preceded scientific thinking. This particular phrasing suggests that these three general explanatory schemes are something more, namely, that they are connected with structures of the mind—that is, the ways in which we think. It is thus tempting to conclude that simple minds think simple things like magic; more sophisticated minds think more sophisticated things like religion; and the culmination of the process is when supremely self-confident Victorian intellectual minds think science.

From this tissue of confusion came all sorts of theories to

33

the effect that primitive peoples were simpleminded, childish, or even not very intelligent. Airs of superiority could thus be adopted toward those who adhered to superstition instead of science. However, as soon as students of human society began to study these primitive peoples carefully—which involved more than just being in contact with them—evidence accumulated that they were in all respects just as intelligent as Europeans. There were differences: being literate makes for higher achievement levels in many areas. But where the basis of comparison was fair there seemed no evidence that savages were stupid or even "savage."

Besides all this, the evolutionary sequence seems just a trifle too cut and dried, too neat. In animal evolution things are much more complicated; there is no simple lineup of one species giving rise to another. Animal evolution is much more like the branching and twisting of a tree with a great many branches off the main trunk. It is difficult to see any parellel in social evolution. Could it then be argued plausibly that magic, science, and religion were equally old, and that magic and religion were left untouched by natural selection (doing no harm to man), and so established themselves while continuing to coexist with other ideas? Why should natural selection leave magic and religion untouched? Perhaps because it is indifferent to them. Provided they do not positively endanger survival they cannot be wiped out because the only way nature has of wiping out beliefs is by eliminating those who hold them. Nature cannot eradicate beliefs as such. Since people have memories and can communicate beliefs, only by extirpating everyone can nature ensure that a belief, like the dodo, becomes extinct. But then obviously beliefs behave differently from species. Human will, memory, and ability to communicate can preserve beliefs, however inefficient, provided they do not actually lead to the death of the society. And even then *these* beliefs can be retained *provided they are not acted on.*

34

But if magic, religion, and science did not evolve one from the other, from where did they come? After all, they coexist in most societies in the West. Did this perhaps suggest that magic, religion, and science were *not* three ways to answer the one question why do certain events, and especially disasters, occur? Were they answers to different questions? The most recent development of a theory of this kind suggests that magic and religion both have a strong element of symbolism in them, spiritual symbolism. The argument is that all cultures have something that is like science: they can all fish, cultivate, grow crops, hunt game, or treat disease. These practical activities are primitive forms of science. But why do they also, as we do not, pray for rain or perform magical rain rituals? The answer given is that they do it to express or symbolize the importance of what they want. A rain dance is a way of getting the whole group together and reiterating as one voice the importance of rain. This is in addition to any feeling they may have that the gods will actually intervene or that the magic will work. Indeed we in the West pray for family and friends, knowing with half our minds that it will not make any difference. Illness or accidental death will come and strike people anyway, and we do not turn around and blame whatever god to whom we have prayed. On the other hand our praying expresses our goodwill toward those we pray for, and focuses our thoughts on them and our love for them. Children's bedtime prayers are a good example.

A contemporary British anthropologist, E. E. Evans-Pritchard, has argued that magic does not so much explain why the crops grow or the rain comes, but explains mysterious events such as why the rain fails to come. Where straightforward explanations are available, primitive man accepts them. If a school of fish congregate in one bend of the river, then he fishes there. He does not perform magic to get them to come where they have never been. He knows that to catch fish you must know where they are. But how does primitive man answer questions such as, why do the fish swim away one day? Why did termites cause my house to collapse and not someone else's? Why did the malaria mosquito bite me and not him? African people such as the Azande of the Sudan, according to Evans-Pritchard, explain these occurrences as the result of the operation of witches. They then try to find out who the witch is and either stop him or direct countermagic at him. The test of witchcraft is to give poison to a fowl; if it lives, it shows magic is present. This magic involves no sorcery of potions and ritual; it is rather a force some people can command and which can be detected only in postmortem examinations.

So far, then, we have reviewed the following attempts to explain the religion of primitive peoples: (1) they are dumb and so don't understand why things happen; (2) they are less evolved and so have not yet figured out why things happen; (3) they are symbolizing in their religion what they consider important, not explaining why things happen; (4) they use magic to explain the workings of luck or fate. This is by no means a complete list of the theories of primitive religion to be found in the history of anthropology. However, those we have picked out are important highlights in that history. Looked at together, they can be seen to share a common feature: all are psychological theories. They trace the origin of religion to the psychological state of primitive man. Theory (1) suggests that because primitive people are dumb they do not know the explanation of dreams, hallucinations, shadows, darkness, and such like, and so have come to believe in spirits, ghosts, demons, and gods. The evolutionist theory (2) says that they make this mistake because they are less evolved rather than because they are dumb. The theory (3) that religion symbolizes for primitive peoples important events (the harvest) and important ideas (morality) again derives religion from peculiarities of primitive thought (they express their thought in symbols, rather than directly). More detailed developments of these theories have been skipped over in our account: the role of *fear* and *superstition* in religion, for example; or Frazer's discussion of magic in terms of the principles of *thought* that like produces like and that things which have once been in contact with each other continue to act on each other at a distance after the physical contact has been severed; or the attempt to show how monotheism (belief that there is only one god) emerged from polytheism (belief in many gods). We have skipped them in order to contrast psychological theories with theories of a totally different kind—sociological theories.

Broadly speaking, the contrast between these two kinds of theories of religion is this. A psychological theory explains religion by some kind of thought or mental process (of figuring out) the primitive people might have gone through. This stresses religion as a system of ideas which have to be thought up. But religion also consists of rituals, observances, prayers, and other actions which people not so much *think,* as *do.* Sociological theories stress this aspect of religion and try to explain the ways these doings connect up with other actions. The most famous sociological theory made its appearance at the turn of the century in the work of the Frenchman Emile Durkheim. He argued that totemic religion, where parts of society associate themselves with an animal which then takes on a semisacred status for them, is an instance of the object of worship being a symbol of society itself. Durkheim wanted a theory of religion which took every religion and its ideas seriously. There must be some truth in every religion. How else could religion be so widespread, so long-lasting? Of course, each religion cannot be literally true because of the very existence of competing, conflicting, contradictory religions. And who could pick the one true one out if there were such? Instead Durkheim seeks the meaning or heart of religion not in its ideas but in its rites. He points out that in all religions there is a coming together of the community or large parts of it to perform rites collectively. He suggests that man depends on society for aid and protection, but that for society to continue as a community, its members must periodically forgather or assemble to reaffirm their ties. In such a forgathering they experience heightened emotional states and in such heightened emotional states they conceive the ideas that constitute their religious doctrine. So what lies behind both the ideas and the gathering together is the social necessity of reaffirming community continuity and solidarity.

Durkheim's theory, however, is a trifle general, and might seem difficult to apply to the myriad different kinds of religion. Yet contemporary anthropologists have tried to do this. They have tried to show that where kinship ties are very significant in a society, then worship of the ancestors will be found. This turned out not to be true. They have tried to show that where a plant or animal is vital to the survival of a people it will have religious beliefs surrounding it. This also turned out not to be true: in India sacred cattle are the people's greatest burden, not their greatest benefit. Sudanese Nuer whose entire lives center around cattle do not at all regard them as sacred any more than Oceanic peoples regard their staple food, yams, as sacred.

Many other theories have attempted to explain religion in general. Karl Marx, for example, suggested it was an instrument for fobbing off or putting aside the discontent of the laboring masses with fairy stories. He thus boldly connected the economic system of society to its belief system and predicted that with the end of economic exploitation and discontent in society, religion would no longer be needed.

Having outlined these various theories of religion and magic it is a temptation to sum up, but this should always be avoided. This subject is neither an easy one nor one on which there is general agreement.

It might seem that our current theories are best. But to

assume this is to make the same mistake as the evolutionists made when they thought that Victorian science was the height of man's mental development. Current theories are as susceptible to error as any previous theories: our ideas do get better and more accurate, but they do not yet approach finality. In the matter of symbolism, for example, it is by no means clear what this sort of theory explains or whether it is supplementary to, or a substitute for, the idea that religion and magic explain the world. Moreover, there is a tinge of relativism in our modern view, and this is highly contentious. In the face of the many religions and ways of life revealed by anthropology, it is difficult to decide which is correct. Sometimes we are tempted to conclude that since a people's beliefs are part and parcel of their way of life they must be correct *for them*. What is correct varies with, is relative to, different peoples and ways of life. This argument can easily lead to ethical relativism, which says truth or goodness is relative: what is good in one society is not in another, so if we ask whether stealing is bad we cannot answer in general, but only relative to a particular society and its unique value system. Religions which advocate killing the nonbeliever would seem on the face of it less desirable than others by most people's standards. A relativist might answer that this argument simply elevates the value of human life above that of truth, and that this emphasis on life may be our value but it is not everyone's. But the issue is not to be arbitrarily decided by the relativist either. It certainly cannot be the case that those who claim life as *the* supreme value and those who claim truth are both correct. That is logically impossible. Relativism says both are incorrect; there is no supreme value, only the values of individuals and societies. But the relativist is caught in his own trap: for *him* there may be no supreme values, but there may be for *me*, if I am not a relativist. Is the doctrine of relativism itself true only relative to a context? Or is it alone absolutely true?

Theories of religion faced with such serious difficulties as these cannot be accepted uncritically. It might seem that while modern ideas are some advance on evolutionism, there are elements in evolutionism which deserve to be preserved. In particular, Frazer's theory, if studied not psychologically but logically, allows that all men, including savages, are rational. They all, he seems to say, grapple with the problem of explaining their world. He thus allows a continuity in man's endeavors. All men have striven to explain and control the world, the savage no less than the scientist. Each of the solutions so far entertained by man was once plausible and worth taking seriously. Even Frazer's optimism that with science the peak of development has been reached should not be taken too literally. In a suggestive passage in his beautiful prose he indicates that the quest for understanding is never-ending:

> Reflection and enquiry should satisfy us that to our predecessors we are indebted for much of what we thought most our own, and that their errors were not wilful extravagances or the ravings of insanity, but simply hypotheses, justifiable as such at the time when they were propounded, but which a fuller experience has proved to be inadequate. It is only by the successive testing of hypotheses and rejection of the false that truth is at last elicited.[6]

[6] Sir James Frazer, *The Golden Bough,* abridged edition, Macmillan, London (St. Martin's Library), 1957, vol. I, p. 348.

CHAPTER TWO

Family and Kinship

IN Chapter 1 we discussed how the study of anthropology in addition to taking us far afield can bring to our attention unfamiliar aspects of, or ways of looking at, quite familiar things like religion. To continue this discussion one stage further, let us consider the history of the anthropologist's study of an even more familiar aspect of the lives of all of us— the family. We are in a family from the moment of birth; so a family is something we have been around a long time, and this is true for every member of every society on earth. Anthropologists regard this very familiar institution as one of the central problems of their science. The general development of their views—from initial incomprehension, through elaborate and ingenious explanations, to some sort of refined but workable ideas—has followed much the same pattern as in the field of religion. But explanations of the details have been much more bizarre, and anthropologists have certainly made considerable progress in understanding the family, whereas it is questionable whether they now have any deeper understanding of religion than did their predecessors.

Of all the many people we come into contact with in the course of our daily lives—friends, neighbors, teachers, shop clerks—none is quite so special a group as our relatives, or, as we sometimes call them, our kith and kin. Mother, father, brother, sister, son, daughter, aunt, uncle, grandmother, grandfather, cousin, grandchild are all family. We rarely see all of them at one time, only at weddings, funerals, christenings, and so on. Within our relatives is a smaller group of those with whom we share a home. For each of us this group—parents, brothers and sisters, maybe grandparents—is the nucleus of our relatives. Anthropologists call it the "nuclear family." *All* our relatives considered as a group are called the "extended family."

Why are relatives something special? In what ways are they special? First of all they surround us. Our home usually is populated by our nuclear family only—our parents, our brothers and sisters. In addition to being around us, our relatives are not easy to get away from. It is difficult for youngsters simply to run away and survive, because they are utterly dependent on the family for money and shelter. Also, if they are caught running away, the police automatically return them to their family, like it or not. However, if a youngster really drops out of sight, what then? Well, his relatives are still his relatives. He may not see them any more, and may not care that he does not see them, but they do not cease to be his relatives nonetheless.

Is there absolutely no way to divest yourself of a family? What happens if your parents die? If you are a minor, you are either sent to an orphanage or adopted by other people, and *they* become your father and mother; not only do you call them that, but you come to think of them that way, and even to *feel* toward them that way. Most adopted children, even after they have been told they are adopted, feel the same way about their adoptive parents as do other children.

Running away or being orphaned aside, relatives, especially close or nuclear relatives, are more or less inescapable. However undesirable, a relative is a relative. The "black sheep" brother or uncle who regularly turns up at all sorts of inconvenient moments to embarrass the family and in between completely drops out of sight, is a standard character in fiction and very real in some family histories. The family ties that bind us to these characters seem to have considerable force. It is bad behavior, for example, to turn away from the door your black-sheep brother even if his need is not acute. We are expected to love, or at least feel a special attachment to, our relatives. Most of us, in fact, love our parents. In our relationship with our brothers and sisters sometimes we are friends, sometimes we quarrel, and sometimes we ignore them. When the bullies appear it is marvelous to have an older brother with a big fist; when bodies or feelings have been hurt or homework is to be done, it is marvelous to have comforting and helpful parents. At such moments our hearts overflow with love, warmth, gratitude toward them.

Having a home and family can make us feel very secure, especially since we know that if we are naughty they will still be there. If we behave badly a friend may drop us; teachers and neighbors do move away from time to time regardless of what we do. Relatives, however, go on being relatives. Sometimes they go on and on and on! And of course, just by going on they can be pests as well, and then they arouse in us emotions quite different from love, warmth, gratitude. Parents who press us to eat our food, wash behind the ears, not interrupt when they are speaking, not ask them to buy things, and brothers and sisters who tease, borrow things, tell tales and so on, do not arouse warmth and love—never mind gratitude—in us. It is nice to have relatives, but they are a pain in the neck sometimes. But if they are a pain in the neck why do we not try to escape them? We do not because we need them. We do escape them temporarily, but our need keeps us from going too far. Children, as soon as they can communicate, spend long hours playing by themselves, away from adults. School, jobs, friends, all serve as an escape from too much family togetherness. Even in the happiest of families people get on each others' nerves and need to get away from time to time. Rare indeed is the individual who leaves home and family before college, a job, or marrying and setting up his own home push him into it.

Let me not give the impression that we are all disgruntled and dying to get away from our parents. The point to stress is that being a member of a family, having relatives, is not merely a matter of being close to some people. Thinking this way might lead one to conclude that after a certain age membership in a family is a voluntary thing. How much you see of your relatives, and how much or how little you love them becomes, it is true, voluntary in adult life. But the physical fact of your relationship by blood to certain people is not voluntary. And, perhaps more important, the legal or, as anthropologists prefer to say, juridical relationships of the family cannot easily be altered. Whatever changes take place in your *social* relationship with your brother, he remains legally your brother and his wife remains legally a relative by marriage. Should you be hurt or should you, being underage, incur a debt, the authorities will contact your next of kin. Who that is, is a legal matter, not a social one. There are legal means whereby an adult can cite others than relatives as next of kin, but these are not foolproof. Inheritance is another case. We all know the stories of lawyers tracking down the lost or remote relatives of a dead millionaire so that his fortune can be passed on.

This net of blood, social, emotional, and juridical ties is especially tight around a young person. An adolescent can marry only with the consent of his legal guardian (usually the father); he cannot enter into contracts or leases of any kind; he has no legal right to live away from home before a certain age, and so on. Society through its laws makes the family responsible for its offspring. This is partly because a newcomer must depend on someone or something.

44

Just who are these relatives on whom we depend? Are they people we feel very close to and call relatives? Or are they people to whom we are related and therefore feel very close to? One answer might be that they are both. Adoptive parents are certainly different from parents because there is no blood tie. The feelings toward them are similar, though; hence we call them mother or father. When you are taught to call your parents' friends "uncle" and "aunt" you know there is no blood relationship, but otherwise you treat them as normal uncles and aunts. The courtesy titles "uncle" and "aunt" are conferred because we behave toward them as if they were blood relatives. When we speak of being estranged from a section of the family or from a sibling (which is a collective noun for brothers and sisters who are children of the same parents) what we mean is that, regardless of blood ties, the person does not behave toward those from whom he is estranged as relatives in that category are normally expected to.

What is the significance of discussing the family and its clutches? Why is there so much concern with relatives—who they are and how they function? The study of relatives and groups of relatives such as families has preoccupied anthropologists for a very long time, and they have discovered some very interesting things. At first they were unable to comprehend the family system of native peoples. In societies where a man had several wives the nuclear family was rather more extensive than ours. Such societies as the Iban of Sarawak do not have a hut for every nuclear family; here, several families share a large one. This arrangement led anthropologists to wonder if there was not a sort of group marriage in these huts, with the children belonging to all the adults collectively. This turned out not to be so. While there are societies where a man has several wives (among desert Arabs, for example), or even where a woman has several husbands (among the Todas of India), group marriage has never in any society been a prevailing type of marriage. Always, the legal and economic responsibility for the children is clearly defined. The Iban, in fact, may inhabit a long house, but the families within it are monogamous, and each one has its own rooms divided from its neighbors by partitions. What was to be made of societies where young men and women left home at puberty and lived together in communal huts before getting married? Variations on this are to be found in Melanesia, where adolescent Trobriand Islanders can live together in the *buku-matula,* or bachelors' and unmarried girls' house; in the Philippines, where boys can visit the girls in their *olag,* or dormitory; in Africa among the Nandi and the Masai, both of Kenya. In the latter case the youths live in a separate village to look after the cattle and they are joined by elder woman and young girls who sleep freely with the youths. Even the way relatives are classified is different from society to society. Every language has words equivalent to father, mother, son, and daughter. But a difference emerges in the language in some societies in expressing the relationships of uncle, aunt, and cousin. We make no distinction between the brothers and sisters of our father, and the brothers and sisters of our mother; all are uncles and aunts. In other societies, however, quite different labels are given to father's brother and mother's brother. Similarly a distinction is made between father's father and mother's father, both of which we merge in the single name grandfather. And while we lose track of our cousins, other societies may have specific words for, for example, mother's father's brother's son's son and father's mother's mother's brother's son's daughter. In our society we call both cousin. There are societies such as the Ganda of Uganda where men avoid being even glimpsed, never mind looked upon, by their mothers-in-law (the custom of mother-in-law–avoidance). In some societies a man feels he belongs as much to his lineage as to his family—a lineage being all his relatives in either the male or female line. His father, his father's brothers, his father's father and *his* brothers, and so on, are a man's patrilineage; his mother, her sisters, his mother's mother and *her* sisters, and so on, constitute a man's matrilineage. (See Diagram A.) Some societies are organized around the patrilineage and are called "patrilineal" (or agnatic), others around the matrilineage and are called "matrilineal." A few others organize around both and are called "double-unilineal." Societies exist where the children and grandchildren of mother's brother are called mother's sister or mother's brother, depending on sex, thus classing several generations together; whereas those of father's sister are called sister's daughter or sister's son. (This is an example of the Omaha kinship-naming system, which the Fox Indians use; see Diagram B.)

The examples could be multiplied endlessly. The question is, how can this great diversity of kinship systems be explained? Only two answers have been given to this question, and they are the same two answers as were given to explain the differences of religious practice mentioned in the first chapter. One explanation involves tracing such diversities back into history; the other involves trying to figure out how a society with a different kinship system works and then seeing if any further explanation is needed. When the second approach was tried seriously what happened was that it came to seem that it was *our* system of naming and classifying relatives that needed explanation. Thus, the queer customs which we began with were puzzling no longer.

The first attempt to explain the way primitive peoples classify their relatives and behave toward them was the theory that, being ignorant and foolish savages, they just were not capable of knowing what they were doing. In other words it was no good looking closely at the way their society worked because it was just a confused muddle anyway, with no rationale. This theory, which we can call the theory of *savagery as a confused muddle,* no doubt inhibited for a long time those who might have been inclined to go and make close

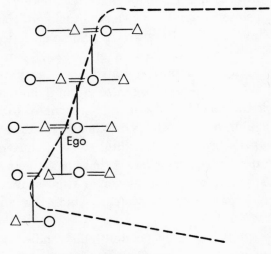

EGO'S MATRILINEAGE

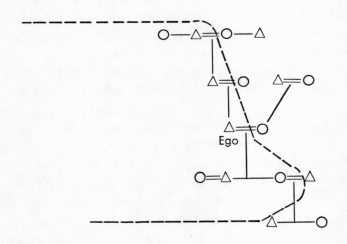

EGO'S PATRILINEAGE

DIAGRAM A
Lineages

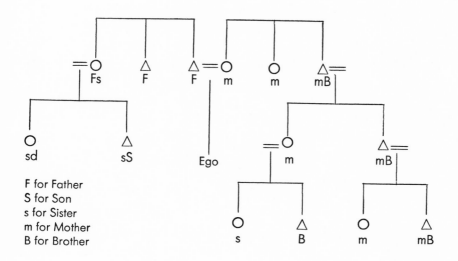

F for Father
S for Son
s for Sister
m for Mother
B for Brother

DIAGRAM B
Omaha Kinship Naming

studies of these seeming oddities. Since there was no reason in such systems, why bother with them? Who could ever explain such a foolish action as grown men hiding the instant their mother-in-law hove into sight?

How was this theory refuted? Very slowly, as closer study was made and one oddity after another began to make sense, the theory was abandoned. It could have been refuted immediately, though, without waiting for evidence. If savages were foolish people who did not know what they were doing, then one would expect no order at all in their social behavior. But the early reports speak of consistent patterns such as dodging mothers-in-law or calling mother's brother's children uncle and mother. Savage society, in other words, shows evidence of reason and orderliness. So the confused-muddle theory was no

49

good from the start: it would explain chaos, but not these consistent patterns of behavior.

Another theory, which has been called the theory of *primitive promiscuity*, was regarded seriously for some time and stated not so much that savages were without reason, but that their society was poorly organized. What was especially important and missing was marriage. Marriage, this theory said, is a sophisticated idea for regulating sexual relationships and the production of children. Savages, however, lived together in hordes, where sex was indiscriminate and children did not know how they were related to people other than their father or mother, and so they named everyone in the mother's generation mother, and so on.

This theory was shown to be false when it was found that there was method in their "madness." For one thing, young people as well as adults are often classed as "mothers" in such societies. No one suggests primitive peoples are so confused or disorganized that they mistake children for parents; there must be reason behind this system of naming. So the question of whether or not primitive peoples had the institution of marriage remained open. (As it turned out, no society on earth is without marriage.)

Both theories had their vogue. They gained much credence from evidence that seemed to show that family institutions existed only vestigially among the Australian aborigines and other very primitive peoples. This evidence was reviewed and reinterpreted by Westermark (1891) and Malinowski (1913) and shown to be in conflict with the facts.[1] The Australian aborigines have in truth a very well-developed and sophisticated system of family and marriage.

Both theories also conflicted with common sense. Even if

[1] Edward Westermark, *The History of Human Marriage*, Macmillan, London, 1891; Bronislaw Malinowski, *The Family Among the Australian Aborigines: A Sociological Study*, University of London Press, London, 1913.

the horde is promiscuous, one relationship must be universally known and recognized: motherhood. (The possible exception of communal rearing is unknown in primitive society. Children may sometimes be raised by a woman other than the biological mother; but there is always one, special, social mother.) How could it be possible that a child, reared for years by his mother, could cease to know her or of her special relationship to him? By extension, the second most clearly marked relationship would be between those acknowledging the same mother, that is brothers and sisters or siblings. This theory we might label the theory of the *primacy of motherhood.* So strong was the impact of this theory that mother-child relations were used to explain the whole development of the human family. Much credence was given the theory since there were family systems which had been uncovered by anthropologists in which women played a very different role from the one they play in our society. In some, such as the Ashanti of Ghana, or the Navaho of Arizona and New Mexico, a man inherits land and property through his mother and is regarded as belonging to his mother's family or *line of descent.* At first anthropologists thought these institutions were part of a matriarchy. A matriarchy is a society ruled at all levels by women—for example, the Amazons of Greek legend who went so far as to drive all men out of their society. It was thought women would more or less run society, being the only fixed points in it, while men clustered around them and dispersed as they wished. Yet this was refuted too: *no social system so far discovered is in any sense matriarchal.* Women do not anywhere rule the whole society, and on the rare occasions when women are chiefs or kings they are in many ways treated as though they were men rather than women—for example they may marry other women, who then have children by an assigned lover, the children belonging to the lineage of the (female) husband. Both the Zulu of South Africa and the Nuer of the Sudan have this custom.

From the point of view of a child, the really powerful, father-figure type in these female-line societies is his mother's brother. So instead of being matriarchal, these systems came to be called matrilineal because the line of descent is through females. Descent is only one factor. If in a society with lineages the three items of descent, inheritance, and succession to office all follow one line, then the society is said to be unilineal. Unilineal systems can be either matrilineal or patrilineal. If one or two of these three items is traced in the alternate line to the other, the society is called double-unilineal.

Thus the questions arise: How can one account for this trifold diversity of kinship systems? Is there any explanation for one society being organized one way, another another way? All sorts of explanations have been tried. Some attempted to connect the organization of a kinship system with its religion, its geographical location, the kind of farming in which its members engaged, and so on. But to pursue these lines requires first of all a greater amount of information about the peoples concerned than was in fact available (not to mention some indication as to whether those facts known were from an unbiased sample). Second, and very important, some *theories* which would make the relation of kinship to religion, geography, or agriculture intelligible were required. Without such theories, explanations linking kinship with such things would never suggest themselves.

Instead, what suggested itself was, as usual, a version of the theory of evolution: these kinship systems had evolved, one from the other. But which from which? The answer seems to be fairly obvious: given the theory of the *primacy of motherhood*, matriliny is the basic system. On the basis of the information he had, the Scottish sociologist John McLennan (1867–1935) thought that matriliny was the prevalent mode of kinship organization amongst rude (that is, unsophisticated) peoples. (This information was mistaken.) Patriliny, which

emphasizes the father and thus presupposes some understanding of the male role in reproduction, seemed to be more
sophisticated and was thus thought to have evolved from
matriliny. Double unilinearity could then be seen as a transi-
tional stage between them, or so the argument went. The version
of the theory of the primacy of motherhood that developed
then was that matrilineal societies arose because to the
simplest peoples only the mother-child relationship was clearly
identifiable. In other words, the most primitive of peoples
were thought to be ignorant of fatherhood, that is, of the role
of the father in reproduction. However, the argument pro-
ceeded, as primitive peoples began better to understand the
nature of fatherhood and as more regularized unions came
about between men and women (approximating marriage),
anthropologists thought that mother-centered societies might
give way to father-centered societies, or patrilineal societies.
Such a theory is buttressed by the convenient existence of
double-unilineal societies, as we have just described, which
can be looked at as representing the transition from female
descent to male descent. (These societies would have to be
observed over a long time to see if they were gradually changing over from one to the other.)

The confusion between matrilineal and matriarchal has
been one of the most persistent in anthropology and was not
resolved until the second quarter of this century. Discussion
of who had the power over children, the father (father-right)
or the mother (mother-right), plagued clarification of these
ideas for a long time. It was difficult for anthropologists to
grasp the idea that although women provided, for example, the
line of descent, they in fact wielded no more power in a
matrilineal society than in a patrilineal one. While descent,
succession, and inheritance might be reckoned through the
blood connection of females, it is quite possible that authority
over descendants, office, and property are controlled by males.
Among the matrilineal Ashanti, the chief is the senior *man* of

the lineage, his relation to the senior woman being that of brother. As such he has the main responsibility for raising his sister's children, for educating them, disciplining them, giving them permission to marry, and so on. Over his own children a man will have relatively little to say.

The difficulty of grasping the workings of such societies is perhaps explained because our own society is neither matrilineal, nor patrilineal, nor double-unilineal, although it was at various times confused with the last two. In our society we do not name our kin like the Fox Indians, nor do we have a patriarchy. Admittedly, women in our society take on their husband's name, swear to love and obey him, and so forth. But in fact, and in law, women are more or less equal to men, and, more important, the relatives on our mother's side of the family are of as much importance as the relatives on our father's side. When we talk of our uncles and aunts we include the brothers and sisters (and their spouses) of both our father and our mother. Eventually, this kinship system we possess came to be called bilateral because it is equally ramified on both the father's and mother's sides. In a double-unilineal system only the father's male relatives and the mother's female relatives are counted as important as members of the family; we, however, count father's male *and* female relatives and mother's male *and* female relatives as constituting the extended family. Nevertheless, attempts were made to explain our system of kinship by saying it was a decayed form of unilineal kinship, better adapted perhaps to conditions in our society. Research, however, has indicated that as far as we can trace back, Anglo-Saxon society did not have unilineal kinship groups. Further checking reveals that in untouched—and otherwise unspectacular or peculiar—societies in Melanesia and Africa similar bilateral kinship may have evolved out of some other prior pattern (or, more likely, vice-versa). But the weight of such other evidence as there is rather goes against this and favors the view that the diverse

54

patterns of patriliny, matriliny, double-unilinearity, and bi-laterality can all be traced back equally far in time. There is, in other words, evidence which refutes the theory that one system is more basic or older than the others, such that the others could have evolved from it, and there is also evidence that supports the theory that no one system is the oldest.

The story of anthropologists' attempts to understand the family and kinship-naming systems does not end with the refutation of the evolutionary theory of kinship. Before we go further, however, let us review the discussion, for the dis-coveries made up to this point are such that the original problems have deepened and ramified quite a bit. We have come across societies with lineages as well as extended and nuclear families, with female descent as well as male, and various combinations of these. And we have added the problem of explaining not only these various systems, but also the diversity of systems itself. This new depth coincided with the adoption of a new theoretical outlook in anthropology. Hitherto primitive societies were treated as pieces of frozen history, that is, as relics to be explained away. All the theories we have discussed assumed that the so-called primitive peoples really *are* historical primitives—that they in some ways resemble our forebears. The evolutionists simply took this assumption seri-ously and went ahead and actually tried to reconstruct the stages on the road to our own development.

A strict evolutionist has to face the question, how have these relics survived? They must provide sufficient protection for their members to allow survival. What needs to be investi-gated, then, is how exactly they provide protection while yet differing very much from most societies with which we are familiar. These are the fundamental arguments which caused anthropology to change so much in this century. As long as anthropology was the study of primitive peoples, as long as the study of primitive peoples was the study of frozen soci-eties from which the history of mankind could be read off, anthropologists were complacent about testing their theories by looking closely at these societies themselves. They were complacent because they already felt they had at hand a great deal of evidence in travel books and in the literature of the Old Testament, Greece, and Rome. They believed that the main task was to make sense of the diverse and bizarre reports from around the world so that the history of man could be seen as leading up to the civilization of Greece and Rome and then onward to Western Europe in an orderly and intelligible fashion.

Today, anthropologists have gone to the other extreme and find all attempts to use anthropology to reconstruct the history of mankind profoundly uninteresting. They claim that these reconstructions cannot be tested, and so their truth or falsity is a matter for speculation. Before there were written records the only possible test evidence we have is provided by archeology, and these outlines of buildings, fragments of tools and crockery tell us nothing about kinship. The breakthrough to modern anthropology came in kinship studies. It is here, above all, that history was replaced by sociology.

Describing accurately what you observe is a very difficult task. Questioned about a picture flashed in front of them, many people will miss, misrepresent, and disagree about what they saw. In the film *Twelve Angry Men* a jury given an open-and-shut case changes its opinion when it transpires that a witness could not possibly have seen what he sincerely claimed to have seen. A layman taken into a school chemistry laboratory and asked to describe the apparatus might speak of tubes, liquids, and wires, thereby missing the point because he does not know what he is looking at or looking for. The trained observer, however, is like the Indian in films who can follow the trail of man or animal for days on the basis of clues we could not even see without lengthy training. Generally, then, the way people see and interpret the facts of the world around them is heavily conditioned by their education and training and, especially, the expectations they have.

No doubt early travelers to savage society had only semi-articulated expectations of what they would find there. They seem to have expected savages to live in a kind of primordial darkness: primitive, unintelligent, superstitious, and perhaps not even capable of communicating with more than grunts. A number of early travelers reported that societies they visited had no language. Included among these were the Singhalese, who in fact have a very highly developed and sophisticated language. As to kinship, these early travelers seem to have expected almost anything. Of course, stories about selling babies, infanticide, human sacrifice, and so on, played their part. The upshot was that until the mid-nineteenth century many observers' reports of the kinship of primitive peoples were pure balderdash, no more reliable than if they had been made up before the traveler set out on his journey. In many cases the travelers didn't know the language of the people (especially when they believed they had none), hadn't the remotest idea that there were alternate kinship patterns to ours (as they *should* have known if they had known the Old Testament or Roman law properly), and were therefore baffled by what they observed or thought they observed. How their preconceptions led them grossly to misobserve is no doubt itself an interesting problem—even an anthropological problem. Be that as it may, what was needed was correction of such misobservation.

Among the Hausa of West Africa, for example, a mother avoids all possible physical contact with her first-born child; does this practice prove that savages do not have even the normal human instincts of love and devotion between mother and child? No wonder they allegedly sell their children into slavery, and so on! This argument is a tissue of mistakes and can be shown to be so. If the Hausa mother has no feelings of love and devotion, then this avoidance of affectionate contact

57

will be accompanied by no signs of distress or strain, and she presumably will act the same with the second-born, third-born and so on. This is not the case. The Hausa mother avoids her baby only with almost superhuman effort and encouragement from her family. But to test in such detail this emotional-deficiency explanation of Hausa motherhood practices, one must know the society quite intimately. One must first of all know the language, and secondly reside among the Hausa in order to observe the mother to see if strain or distress shows, to question her about her feelings, to see if she acts similarly toward all her children and, most especially, to work oneself into a position of trust where one can ask, why this alienation? Do Hausa explain this behavior as completely natural and straightforward or as some special quirk? (See following pages.)

In other words, the misrepresentations of savage society cannot be properly cleared up, cannot be thoroughly tested without going there for extended, close study, an expedition into the field known as *fieldwork*. Fieldwork is something that has really changed anthropology. Previously anthropologists never even dreamed of getting close enough to savages to study them in detail. There were those in government, church, or business who were living in close proximity to savages, but they did not do anthropological fieldwork. British colonizers often lived in Africa and India for many years; yet they returned to their homeland with even worse misrepresentations and travesties of the lives of the people among whom they had been living than the ones they had set out with. Fieldwork is more than just knowing the language, living among the people, and much more than establishing the right kind of relationship. Perfectly amicable but quite noncommunicative relationships are possible. There have to be two things further: first, a spirit of empathy, of trying to see things from the point of view of the people being studied. This involves assuming that they are intelligent and sensible people who do in fact have a point of view that is coherent and understandable to us. The great difference between modern anthropology and anthropology up to the mid-nineteenth century is this new assumption: the lives of savages make good sense if only we know how to get at that sense. Second, the investigator must be a trained observer; he must know what to look for. He must have some acquaintance with the facts of human diversity and of how in other societies these connect and make sense. He must know the right questions to ask; if he is studying the kinship system, for example, he must be able to map its main features in such a way that it can be compared with other systems.

This sort of anthropology began, interestingly enough, in America, particularly with the stimulus of the Bureau of Indian Affairs and the Smithsonian Institution. Among the pioneers was Lewis Henry Morgan whose exploration and exposition of the *League of the Iroquois* (1851) was a fantastic exercise in overcoming prejudice and ignorance. His approach presented "dangerous" savages as living, thinking, rational human beings. Morgan carried out extensive interviews with an interpreter on all aspects of life and culture and was able, in the end, to draw a very full picture of a way of life which he hoped would encourage a kinder feeling toward the Indians.

Morgan's work was continued in subsequent years in America. Fieldwork may have been a fashionable thing to do where Red Indians were concerned; it was far from fashionable where Africans, Polynesians, or even Hindus were concerned. Scholars did not at once conclude from the fact that American Indian society made sense that therefore Australian aboriginal society made sense also. While fieldwork was done, it was not yet believed to be essential to serious anthropology. Then in the 1890s, Franz Boas did fieldwork in Baffin Land (Canada) and British Columbia, and Alfred Haddon led a British expedition to the Torres Straits in Australia. The notion of fieldwork fully crystallized in the experience of Bronislaw Malinowski during the First World War, when he spent several years in the field, much of it living in a tent in Melanesian villages. Interpreters were dispensed with, and the fieldworker tried to enter into the daily life of the native society—speaking their language, eating their food, participating in their rituals and routines. Only in this way, Malinowski reasoned, could the anthropologist get a complete picture of the native society and its principles of operation; hence the stress, associated with fieldwork, on concrete contemporary sociology rather than speculative evolutionary history.

Against the background of field studies of societies as they are, let us look again at some of the questions which were originally answered historically. What is the explanation of the Hausa woman avoiding contact with her first-born? First extra facts have to be dug out. *Both* parents are expected to avoid as much as possible their first-born, and both child and parents must always refer to each other in the third person: child of my husband, child of my wife, wife of my father, husband of my mother, respectively. So strong is this avoidance that after birth a mother has to be ritually compelled to touch her first-born and begin to suckle it. The first question to ask is what *could* explain such customs or what *could* in general explain such avoidance patterns? One answer would be what the people themselves say in explanation of what they do. But people sometimes rationalize (that is, justify themselves after the event); and sometimes they are inarticulate. Another way would be to argue that since this pattern is part of a smoothly running society it must either contribute to that smooth running or, at least, not greatly interfere with it.

Along these lines one could give the following explanations:

(1) This is a Muslim society where women are subordinate to men. Thus an avoidance pattern developed by men could easily be extended to women. Now why would there be an avoidance pattern of the first-born among the men? Very simple; the first-born is the first member of the new genera-

tion, the generation which comes to replace the senior generation, and as such its existence is a threat. Nevertheless, it is
the human and societal duty of parents to care for and raise
their children. Thus we might argue that after initial avoidance of what they find threatening they increasingly come to
terms with their responsibilities as their children multiply:
they avoid the first, the second less so, the third still less, and
so on.

(2) Parents and children are always in conflict. Some psy-
chologists hold that these conflicts originate in very early
childhood. A child, it is said, gets favored treatment by his
parent of the opposite sex: a boy by his mother, a girl by her
father. Strong attachment develops, to the extent that the
child may even feel jealous when the parents are affectionate
toward each other. While these sentiments are universal, the
way a society copes with these feelings of jealousy (and also
guilt about this jealousy) in the child may be unique. We
attempt to cope with childish jealousy by reassuring the child.
Hausa parents might be said to be avoiding inducing jealousy
by not favoring the child with affection. Perhaps as more children are born they lose their will to do this, or they come to
think it unnecessary.

(3) Hausa believe that the first child, while much desired,
in some way brings danger; thus they have developed an avoidance relationship which wards off the danger. This danger is
thought of as stemming, like witchcraft, from close and persistent contact. Moreover, in the process of growing up and
learning about what is what in society these ideas of danger
are handed on unchallenged from generation to generation.
Even the skeptical Hausa can only play it safe by not experi-
menting.

And so on. It is not so very hard to provide theories of sorts.
But the question is whether they explain anything. We might
label Theory 1 a *functional explanation*, since it says that the
function of the avoidance of the first-born is to avoid social

conflict between the new generation and the one it is to succeed. We might label Theory 2 a *psychological* explanation since it traces the avoidance back to underlying psychological conflicts between child and parent which are ameliorated by mutual avoidance. We might label Theory 3 a *logic of the situation* explanation, since it begins by trying to understand how the Hausa see the situation; then it goes on to assert that, from their point of view, the avoidance custom is a logical or rational move given the situation.[2]

These three kinds of explanation are found constantly in current works of anthropology because they were all developed at about the same period (the first two decades of this century) and are not necessarily mutually exclusive. Quite possibly all three given above are true. We will not discuss their respective merits, but try to use them to throw some light on kinship generally and in particular on the family and the emotions and relations which cluster around it.

Two main questions are these: Who are your relatives, and why do you group several of them under one name, while others have a unique name, for example uncle and father? Both questions look a bit silly at first. But they can come alive very quickly. Do you count among your relatives your mother's brother's wife's sister's husband? Your mother's brother's wife is your aunt, clearly a relative, but what about your aunt's sister, and then what about that sister's husband? Americans would not count that man as any relation at all. Now what makes us draw the line of family relationship at mother's brother's wife? She is married to someone with a blood relationship to us, but has none herself until she has children; then, since her children have blood relation to us, and she has blood relation to

[2] Functional explanation of avoidance is expounded in A. R. Radcliffe-Brown, *Structure and Function in Primitive Society*, The Free Press, Glencoe, Ill., 1962; psychological explanation in Sigmund Freud, *Totem and Taboo*, Moffat, Yard, New York, 1918. Situational explanation is applied to avoidance relationships for the first time in theory 3, above.

them, she indirectly has blood relationship to us. There are blood relatives and the spouses of blood relatives, and our kinship trace stops, it seems, at one relative beyond the blood ties (see Diagram C).

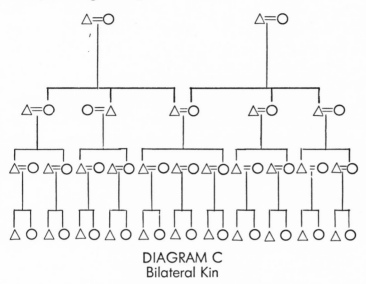

DIAGRAM C
Bilateral Kin

Another way of defining your relatives is by saying that they are all the people you cannot marry. But that is not quite so, because whom you can marry varies from state to state, although the kinship system stays the same. Marriage between first cousins, for example, is prohibited in most states, but legal in California, Connecticut, Florida, Georgia, Kentucky, Maine, Maryland, Massachusetts, New Jersey, New Mexico, Rhode Island, South Carolina, Tennessee, Texas, Vermont, and Virginia. Oklahoma bans marriage between second cousins; no other state does so. In the matter of marriage to stepmothers, stepdaughters, wife's grandmother or granddaughter, son's wife, grandniece and grandaunt, the law varies from state to state, as any good reference book on the law of marriage will show.

In most Western countries a man's brother's wife is counted

as some sort of relative (sister-in-law); yet if his brother dies he can marry her.

Let's try another approach to relatives. Look first not at kinship ties but at the household, the group of people whom you find living together under one roof, the family. These people, as we have seen, can be called the nuclear or elementary family. They are certainly relatives. Now consider the broader group of people you would feel obliged to invite to your wedding, for example. This group can be called your kith and kin. In our society are there any bigger groups of relatives? No, but in other societies there *are* bigger groups, principally the *lineage*. This is an odd sort of group; there is nothing at all like it in our society. Anthropologists were puzzled by lineage for a long time. Once they learned to understand it they began to look on our kinship system in a new way. The lineage is a group of relatives based on a line of descent, those to whom one is related by blood. We in this society think we are related by blood to, or descended from, our father *and* our mother, our grandparents on both sides. We have biological theories about blood ties to confirm this belief. This idea is in contrast to many of the societies studied by anthropologists, where the idea of descent is confined to one sex: our father, his father, his father, and so on, or our mother, her mother, her mother, and so on.

Among North American tribes and peoples in Africa, Oceania, and Southeast Asia, where the lineage is the principal unit of kinship after the nuclear family, much of the social life of the people centers around the lineage. On occasion whole villages will consist of several lineally related nuclear families; at other times the lineage members are dispersed among several villages and never meet together. Nevertheless people may center their religious activities on the founders of the lineage, may regulate who can marry whom and where the newlywed couple shall live, and reckon the inheritance of land and property in terms of their membership in a lineage.

64

If the lineage is the group through which a man gains his inheritance, to which his children belong, and which forbids intermarriage of its members (lineage exogamy), then it makes sense that children are said to be descended from their father and his father, and not from their mother at all. Their mother is simply regarded as the means by which the father (the lineage) has ensured the continuance of his descent line (its existence). Any marriageable woman could have done the job, but the child has only one father, one grandfather, one line of descent, one lineage. Lineage, then, is the name given to all those people who are connected to one line of descent. Girls, of course, will marry the men of other lineages and, where the lineage is the basis of village association, may set up house in their husbands' area. They are not then owned by that lineage, but, on the other hand, their capacity to bear children and to do work does belong to the lineage.

Lineages then can be small groups of people in a village, or they can be huge, dispersed groups ramifying over many miles of territory, depending on the society and its surroundings. These lineages can be traced either through the male line or the female line. This latter is something alien to our society, where descent is *never* traced through mother and mother's mother, and so on. When this matriliny was first discovered, anthropologists assumed that they had come across societies in which women ruled things. As previously mentioned, they expected to find parallels to the legendary Amazons, that society of fierce lady warriors who admitted men to their society only occasionally for breeding purposes. This sort of matriarchal setup turned out to be a myth; in fact power in these matrilineal societies is wielded effectively by men, not the fathers and grandfathers of children, who would not belong to the same lineage, but brothers of the women through whom the line of descent *is* traced. The husbands of women count less because they are not of the blood nor do they belong to the descent line of the matrilineage into which their children are born. They belong to the lineage of their mothers and sisters, where they exercise authority.

In societies which have them, these lineages act just as large corporations do in our society—they act like General Motors, for example. They own land; there are more and less powerful people within the organization; the interests of the organization tend to override those of any of its component individuals should the two conflict; the organization is hierarchical from the executives down to the workers, from the senior to the junior employees. Moreover, in law, General Motors is treated like a person; that is, it can be sued, prosecuted, and so on. And finally, General Motors sometimes controls a whole local group, as in a company town, where everyone in the town either works for GM or is in some way dependent on it (for example, the stores' customers are GM employees). In other places, such as Detroit, GM is just one of a number of corporations in a city. Except for cases where a single town contains a whole division of the company, everyone in GM is never collected together at one place to meet and act in common. Yet despite the dispersion of the corporation it acts in an orderly way in defense and pursuit of its interests.

Let us compare General Motors Corporation with the patrilineage as it operates among the Nuer, a tall and fiercely proud people who dwell, stark naked, around the upper reaches of the Nile. The first great difference is that not only do Nuer lineages never congregate together, but there is no headquarters for Nuer, Nuer tribes, or Nuer lineages. Only when a Nuer of one lineage gets into a quarrel with a Nuer of another lineage is the lineage membership mobilized. But again, the members are never mobilized the way an army is, that is, gathered together at a depot and lined up for the conflict.

Nevertheless, Nuer lineages have a definite corporate personality, if not a corporate image. They control a definite piece of territory, and a man belongs to a lineage more than the lineage belongs to him. For example, if he dies, then the children his wife bears belong to the lineage. His widow cannot return to her home with the children unless her husband's lineage agrees. When cattle were paid by her husband's family to her family at the time of marriage, those were seen as paying for the husband's lineages rights over her children. The number of cattle needed were raised, like a bank loan, from among closely related members of the bridegroom's lineage, and each contributing relative thus has a stake in the transaction—if one can look on a marriage in this way.

None of this quite applies to General Motors, or does it? True enough, GM does have central direction, a headquarters. But GM is never all assembled in one place; only headmen, or executives, ever congregate together. Moreover, there are divisions and rivalries within GM, just as among Nuer tribes and lineages. The different divisions (Chevrolet-Oldsmobile, Pontiac-Buick, Cadillac, Trucks) are friendly rivals; the different regions of the country compete in sales; the many subsidiaries have some independence. Only when there is an external threat are ranks closed and loyalties called upon. Against Ford, or American Motors, or foreign competition, GM mobilizes. Then all regions, all subdivisions, all subsidiaries, fight the enemy tooth and nail, although again they are not marshaled at depots and put in battle order. If battles take place they are organized by those on the spot, as with Nuer. GM, though, does not own women's childbearing and other such rights.

For a joke, let us press the analogy. A Nuer gets much of what he gets from his lineage; it almost owns him rather than vice versa. GM employees are in a similar position. Their livelihood, which is almost everything, comes from GM. How far does it 'own' them? No one person dominates GM, it dominates the people in it. The organization man, the man dedicated to and molded by the organization he serves, is an exaggeration, not a myth. Moreover, to achieve success in an organization like General Motors above certain levels a man's choice of wife become very important. Much of the frisson in such books and movies as *The Organization Man, The Man in the Gray Flannel Suit, A Woman's World,* and *Executive Suite* comes from the realization that the company has a stake in whom a man marries. If he marries a woman who helps, not hinders, his work; is an asset, not a distraction; is a good hostess, not a slattern; is socially adept, not gauche; then, other things being equal, he improves his chances of success. An organization does not, however, *possess* a man's children; or does it? This does not apply to GM, certainly. But the army, for example, is another corporate organization and another matter. The army runs a whole special school system on military lines to receive the children of deceased army men, and the traditions of the army are so strong that the existence of families or dynasties of army officers is something to be taken for granted. True, the army, unlike the Nuer lineage, has no *legal* rights over children, but intriguing parallels are to be found nevertheless.

After this long excursion exploring the idea of strange groups called lineages, we can now return and use it to compare the three kinds of explanation—functional, psychological, and situational logic—which were used in discussing the Hausa avoidance pattern. The problem presently at hand is kinship-naming systems. After the various simple-minded historical explanations mentioned earlier, this century has seen three new assaults on questions of kinship along the lines of these three categories of explanation.

Let us begin with the functionalist. A functionalist explanation of kinship might use the following argument: Everything in a society has been evolved over time, and, like a mutation in an organism, must have persisted because it contributed to, or at least did not inhibit, the survival of the species. This indicates that one should look for explanations of family organization, for example, in the functions it performs:

mainly economic and as a means of social organization. Thus it might be argued that human children need to be looked after by adults for several years after birth, and the family is the economic and social institution best suited to do this. The functionalist explanation of the custom of calling several relatives by the same names as mother or father was formulated by a twentieth-century British anthropologist, A. R. Radcliffe-Brown.[3] His argument is this. What does this extended naming signify? If I'call the friends of my parents uncle and aunt it is not because I have confused them with my real uncles and aunts. It is rather because I treat them as I do uncles and aunts. We have a friendly, relaxed relationship, with no deference as with parents or grandparents, but also without the easy equality we adopt with cousins. So, the argument goes, in a matrilineage the brother of my mother is the male member of the lineage immediately superior to me, charged with overseeing my upbringing and initiation into husbandry, farming, fishing, or hunting (whatever the means of gaining a livelihood). Then it is reasonable to call him father. The argument says that the social relationships the society permits with the people we name determines the name we give to them. They will be given the name also given to the person who has the most similar social relationship: similar relationship, similar name.

However, this functionalist explanation of kinship classification does not work. The Hausa custom of avoidance of the first-born, followed by a rather formal parent-child relationship thereafter, is not extended into the naming system: the first child addresses his mother and father indirectly, but not by names such as he would use to other persons in a formal relationship to him (grandparents, uncles, and so on). Moreover, this Hausa avoidance decreases in intensity with the second, third, fourth child, but the naming does not change

[3] A. R. Radcliffe-Brown, *Structure and Function in Primitive Society*, The Free Press, Glencoe, Ill., 1952.

accordingly. Therefore, it is not a case of similar relationship, similar name.

The psychological explanation of kinship names might proceed from the idea that the family embodies and organizes some elementary psychological feelings everyone has built into them, namely love of father and mother, to the suggestion that there has been a gradual extension and generalization of these emotional ties to siblings, aunts and uncles, and so on. Some have argued that even extended naming patterns follow patterns of sentiment, or of association. We call people aunt or uncle, father or mother, who are not such, because we wish to feel toward them as we feel toward the real thing. This explanation, however, is superficial, because such patterns of sentiment follow social lines outward to relatives, but the relationship precedes the sentiments to which they are attached, and so social things can be assumed to come first. Moreover, the sentiments can be irrelevant to the nature of the relationship. A man may hate his father, but he is not expected to extend that hate to all the other men he calls father. The psychological sentiments can be explained by the social relationship, and so the social phenomenon of naming needs no psychological explanation.

Finally let us come to an explanation which employs situational logic, which is a sociological explanation that is not functional. The family is an institution which organizes people in society in certain ways. Children have to be raised and the family is one way to do this; alternatives are community nurseries or rearing by the old people. However, the family is also a well-entrenched social institution that works very well and constantly reinforces itself by binding our emotions as well as our economic survival in its tentacles (the head of the family is often the sole means of support of the members). Well-entrenched institutions have this self-serving character of being able to engender attitudes of support toward themselves. Unless someone comes up with a better idea, a proposal for reforming society which catches people's imagination, we can expect the family to continue. But let it not be forgotten that, just as the authority of the family is being eroded in the West by the increasing role of the school in education, by the influence of the child's peer group and its subculture in behavior and values, by the availability of divorce, by the social and economic acceptability of male and female bachelorhood, and by the advocates of free love, so in, for example, Africa, the family and the lineage is threatened by the growth of towns and the industrialization of the economy. The traditional supports of the lineage—economic, social, and religious—are threatened by peoples' preference for working in factories rather than owning land and raising cattle or crops, for schools and political parties rather than individual child-rearing and personal initiation ceremonies, for Christianity and Islam rather than the old ideas of spirits and witches. No one need make any intentional assault on the family or the lineage system for it to undergo severe disruption. Detribalization in Africa is precisely such a case: the whole network of traditional social relations is ill-adapted to life in towns and in a money economy. Without consciously knowing it, in choosing to associate with the new ways of life the Africans are contributing to the severe limitation and modification, perhaps even demise, of the old one.

What then about Hausa avoidance and the extension of kinship terms? Hausa believe the first-born is a dangerous person; a dangerous person is to be avoided, or at least kept at a safe distance. Each succeeding child is less of a threat and can be associated with more freely. It makes sense for people to act on things they believe; if Hausa believe first-born are dangerous, it makes sense for them to act on this. On the extension of kinship terms the historical, functional, and psychological explanations all fail. Maybe this is because various questions are mixed up. Why these terms are used in this manner might be a historical question that is unanswerable; it might be a question comparing two societies; it might ask how such names make sense, and this has been answered by the functionalist. In summary, it might be enough to say kinship names are the custom of the people and that they make good sense and have nothing to do with confused minds. Beyond this, the reasons for this kinship practice remain unknown.

Such a logic-of-the-situation account also explains the importance and interest of kinship to anthropologists. Whereas in our society kinship is one among many social institutions, useful mainly in connection with relations between the sexes, the formation of households, and the raising of children, in primitive societies it has a much broader role. In our society the individual owns land and property and he can legally will that it be inherited by whomsoever he wishes. In many lineage societies, land, which is the only wealth, belongs to the lineage and cannot be passed out of it. We have a money economy, where skill and luck, as well as family influence, help one get jobs. In a lineage society the amount of material success one can achieve by individual effort or initiative is relatively slight. Men follow in the footsteps of their father or their mother's brother whether they do it well or not. This perhaps explains why kinship, which is a whole system of statuses and roles ascribed to the individual willy-nilly, is relatively atrophied in our society.

To conclude this chapter let us connect the differences between the way we order our kinship and the way other societies do. A lineage is a way of ordering our kin relations, of controlling the way the society is. Let us again consider General Motors and the Nuer lineage, where there are many parallels, but also some differences. Consider the question of social control, that of maintaining law and order. GM does not undertake this role except in a very limited way on its own premises; the job is delegated to the police. Now the Nuer lineage is a form of police. Your lineage co-members must come to your aid when you are in dispute with a member of another lineage. Again, GM, except in company towns, is only one of a number of alternative means of gaining a livelihood. Nuer lineages control both cattle and cultivable land; other means of livelihood do not exist in Nuerland. GM does not have any very significant religious functions; in the towns there are churches and priests. Nuer kinship is intimately tied in with religious rites, which are always performed in kin groups of one size or another.

With these glaring differences, why draw parallels between GM and Nuer lineages at all? The answer is simple but not quickly explained. GM and Nuer lineages are large-scale social institutions. Social institutions are the key to understanding the way societies work, not only other societies, but our society too. Anthropology is exciting not just because of the bizarre and exotic societies it studies, but also because from those societies we can learn to look again at our own society and discover that we do not know it half as well as we think we do, and that there are things in it that are hard to explain. So in the next chapter we are going to come to the whole question of what societies are all about and see how, despite profound differences between them, they are fundamentally tools, human inventions for coping with the environmental and social problems with which man finds himself faced.

CHAPTER THREE

Social Control

HUMAN societies are very diverse: they worship different gods and have widely differing notions of who is a relative. It is always difficult to understand the ways of those different from ourselves. These diversities occur not only among people from different societies, but also within each society. In the present chapter we will look at the problems created by the differences between individual men. These become problematic in a very straightforward way. Most of us wish to live comfortably and enjoy ourselves; we may not want to live the quiet life, for example, if we are adventurous, but we do not want to be in danger or in a state of constant conflict as we go about our ordinary business either. In the main, it is organized society itself which guarantees that we can enjoy reasonable safety and comfort, the mechanism which both controls men and protects them. Governments make laws which forbid certain things; they pay a police force to enforce their laws and protect people.

Anthropologists have always been impressed on the one hand by the ingenuity of man in creating so many diverse forms of society and on the other by the precariousness of what man has created. Why be impressed? Because men are *so* very different; their desires and needs, their training and standards bring them into constant conflict over land, property, women, power, and so on. If two men want the same piece of land they are in conflict; if one tries to impose his will on the other and the other resists, there is conflict; if they both want to buy the same thing they are in conflict; if they both love the same woman, there is conflict. Bargaining, compromising, bribing, and fighting are means for resolving these conflicts. The conflicts are inherent in the human social situation: living close together and being very different from each other, men sooner or later get onto collision courses. Some would claim conflict and competition are natural in social animals and that society puts men in chains. This makes no sense. Society is natural to social animals and serves a purpose among them. Society ameliorates the worst and most destructive kinds of conflict, and thus promotes that social cooperation which is the key to man's survival. Although society succeeds by and large in holding men in check, anarchy, or the breakdown of controls, constantly threatens because society has not changed the fundamental, conflict-prone situation in which man finds himself. As we shall see later, there are those who have argued that society does change man himself, and for the worse. Be that as it may, the question of how society controls men, what the ultimate basis of its power over us is, how stable that control is, are central to social anthropology. We need to explore further this whole notion of social control before we discuss its history.

So far we have painted a picture of free individuals in conflict being checked or controlled by the rules of the society in which they live. But man is not a loner, he is a social animal; that is, he works together with his fellows in society as an essential part of his way of life, of his means of survival. This has led to the view that man is the way he is *because of* society, not despite it. Controls are not here to check conflict; conflict arises within the framework of controls. Put more shortly, man is viewed by some thinkers as *asocial* rather than social. If man is asocial, individual, anarchistic in outlook at base, then ordered society can be explained as a system of controls he has imposed upon himself in order to ensure his survival. If man is social by nature, however, it is not the creation of ordered society that needs explanation, but deviation and individualism—how it is that man comes to look upon life in society not as something fixed and given, but rather as a convenient way of ordering things that might be altered and made more convenient.

The view that man is asocial sees men as yielding up their freedom and power to society, and obeying its rules for the collective good. The view that man is social says that man could not be what he is, indeed could not be anything, without society, and that such freedom and power as he has are given to him by society in a strictly circumscribed way. Should he abuse this freedom, it can be withdrawn from him again.

Clearly there are seeds here for a very deep and protracted dispute, one liable to infect all discussions of social power, authority, government, and law. The dispute was already present in Ancient Greece, and is with us in the 1970s.

From the very start of the discussion, two positions seem to have been present on the question of the power of society. One is that society is an entity with its own powers and aims which are something over and above those of its members. A man might want to commit a robbery, but in the interests of all, society does not permit him to do so. Possibly each one of us wants to do something which society does not permit—in our general interest. People seem to be both subject and beholden to society for what it offers (protection) and must ultimately knuckle under to its demands if they wish to continue to get such benefits. The other view, while always conceding the power of society, insists that society is and must be the servant of its members; it must not make them beholden; it must not be regarded as something with aims and interests over and above those of its members; and where individual and social interests clash, individual interests which do not harm other people must be allowed to override. Harsh criticism of the society may, for example, be widely resented. However, criticism should not be suppressed, because the individual right to freedom of speech is more important than the dislike of what is said.

Whatever the reasons, most of us are agreed on the necessity for preventing crime and allowing free speech. Where the shoe pinches is in matters like taxation: should society be allowed to take away our wealth in a proportion it decides and to everyone's resentment and spend it for the greater good? In primitive societies this sort of problem shows itself in other ways. When a beast is killed for food, is it right that certain persons always get certain parts of the meat, depending on what kinship relation they hold to the hunter, or should each person get what he wants, or what he needs most?

The first view, which tends to see society as a whole, as a superperson with aims and interests, can be called "holism." The second view, which above all denies that society is a person and restricts that notion to human individuals, is called "individualism." The history of anthropology, sociology, and even political thought can be written as a dialogue between these two competing doctrines.

They clash most basically over the subject of social control —the way society controls its members. The holists seek the legitimacy of control in the interest society has in ensuring its own smooth running and survival and thus benefiting the individual in the long run. The individualists insist that social control is legitimate only if the individuals in the society benefit by it, and individual interests must prevail where they clash with the direction the society is taking.

We can now use these ideas to give a better answer to the general question of why anthropologists are so very interested in family and kinship. The answer is, family and kinship are mechanisms for organizing social relationships, means of social control. People have to live together in society. How should they do this? Well, their biological relations of kinship are a good basis. They are thus grouped together and tied together. Parents have to look after children, stronger after weaker, and so on. Getting food, raising children, building shelter are more efficiently and more effectively done if people cooperate and coordinate their efforts. But how is coordination to be managed? How are conflicts to be resolved? It is done by the rules built around family and kinship. The family does some very important jobs along these lines. Above all, it brings men and women together in a stable emotional relationship out of which come children. The family is a framework within which adults can achieve their aim of raising children; children can achieve theirs of being raised. The family is also a housing arrangement and an economic arrangement, since most housing in the world is family housing, and heads of families usually support their families economically. They may support others also, but this is generally in addition to their families.

The situation then is this. Human beings are creatures who live together in groups we call societies. They do this because of the various things they aim to do: eat, reproduce, worship, defend themselves, talk, sing, dance, create, make friends. Most of these events can be managed in a much more satisfactory way in the framework provided by society than outside it. In fact some of the aims cannot be achieved at all without a society, for example, making friends. To make friends demands at least two people, and when there are two people there is a social relationship, and when there is a social relationship there is in rudimentary form a society. One can put this differently and say that our ancestors are certainly something like monkeys. Most monkeys are already social animals, cooperating and working together in group living, maintaining lengthy attachments between males and females, and devoting considerable care to the rearing of children and even to mourning the dead. This much of society was with human beings when they, so to say, came down from the trees. Society is not an accidental accretion, but an essential feature of the way mankind lives.

We are not forced, however, to accept holism. We might acknowledge that it is true that much of what man is he owes to society, but since society is an abstraction he does not have toward it any obligations such as those he has toward his fellow human beings. And while it is false that man is a free individual oppressed by society, it might be useful to adopt as a moral view that in the interests of his individuality man has a moral right to scrutinize and resist the society wherever he sees fit. Where this right does not impinge on the rights of others, the best society will leave him be; where he does impinge, it will intervene. We cannot be what we are without society; this does not mean that we have to approve of everything in society and accept every change that comes about. Organized society has an inherent tendency to become oppressive, and we are blessed with a moral conviction that this should be resisted.

For purposes of study a number of different facets of society can be distinguished. Among these are those facets that center around marriage and the bearing of children—what we call family and kinship. Others include those centered around beliefs about how the world is made, what causes things to happen, the nature of man, his life and his death, and the explanation of disease and disaster, spirits and gods. These facets are called religion or ritual (see Chapter 1). Still other facets of society are those involved in gaining food; constructing shelter, tools, and implements; making and adapting kinds of costumes; and so on. These involve technology. There are many other facets, but we shall consider the most interesting ones from the point of view of understanding the differences between other societies and our own. The question

of individual differences, their control, harmonizing and chan-
neling has been the central theme of our whole discussion:
how to understand man's diversity. So the facets of societies I
discussed in this chapter are those grouped under the loose
name social control. As this may still sound rather more
vague than it is, although the words are familiar enough,
perhaps the best approach is to illustrate it further with what
we have already learned about family and kinship.

In addition to the other things they are and do, family and
kinship, as we have seen, are mechanisms of social control.
That is, they influence and even *control* the actions people
take. For example, it is usually in the family that children are
taught how to behave and how not to behave. The fact that
they learn from their family not to steal is a clear case of the
family exercising control over them, just as Fagin's teaching
of the Artful Dodger and Oliver Twist to be pickpockets was
his way of exercising control over them. The family's control
(not Fagin's) is called social control simply because the
family is not doing the controlling for its own sake. The family
might itself benefit from everyone in it stealing, but if all
families did this no one would work and eventually there
would be nothing to steal. Fagin is not exercising social control, but control in his own interests, which happen to be
inimical to society's.

Does this look like a strange way to talk of control? It is
not control the way a pilot controls an airplane, or is it?
Well perhaps it is not so dissimilar as all that. The difference
mainly is that the pilot consciously pushes a lever and the
airplane responds. The family does not push any levers to
stop stealing. What the family does is raise the child, teach
or indoctrinate him in how to behave, and thus controls him
in advance and often deliberately. Sometimes we say: "Don't
stick your nose into other people's business or it will grow
longer and longer." This is a joke; but quite often parents
teach or train their children because they believe that unless

80

they do the children will grow up ill-suited for adult life or will not be up to required standards. People look at a child and say: "He is spoiled, *he needs more discipline*," or, "Poor thing, he seems so shy, *he should be encouraged more*." These things are said by *members* of the society and the family, not by the family or the society, because the family or the society are social entities, and, unlike persons, cannot say anything. Nevertheless, add up all the influences and teachings of the various members of your family and society and you can call these the controls family and society have built into you.

On top of these controls the family *can* actively push levers —rather like the pilot. We call these sanctions. When a rich boy brings an unsuitable girl home to present to the family, the family members may hold a meeting to decide what they can do. They can ostracize the couple if they marry, they can all disinherit them, and so on. In traditional China the family was controlled by the oldest living member; this old man or woman, if he was displeased and wished to do so, could make a child an outcast from the society at large, not just from the family.

Thus the family does exercise control over its children. But there is a difference between control and social control: social control means either control by the society or control in the interests of society. Parents try to raise children so that they will be able to make their way in society. Thus, what it takes to make one's way in society is imposed on the child, rather than the child forcing society to let him make his own way. Society has a vested interest in not being challenged and upset. Parents who teach their children not to upset the applecart are controlling them to foster this vested interest. The family rejecting the unsuitable girl is favoring the continuance of that society where girls are invidiously divided into suitable and unsuitable. Society defends itself and controls potential rivalries with these assists from parents and families.

The family, however, is only one mechanism of social control. Religion is another. Social control, after all, involves the prevention of doing harm—to others and to the society as a whole. Religion also prevents such harm. For example, most religions have attached to them lists of prohibitions against certain acts, against certain views, against certain foods, and so on. In our society both robbery and murder are extremely socially destructive, and we as a society want as little of them as possible. Religion strongly discourages both by adding divine punishments to those the state already threatens. These legal and religious proscriptions help to regulate the society. If they did not exist, quite possibly everyone would behave just as he desired, and if everyone behaved just as he desired without regard for others, the strong and the bullies would come out on top, the rest of us would go under, and the society would become one of the most grotesque imaginable.

Of course, neither the family nor religion were in any sense designed to perform these jobs of social control. They nevertheless do this as a by-product of their existence—in the case of the family, its existence as a procreative and economic unit; in the case of religion, as a system of beliefs in other worlds (heaven) and ultimate purposes (salvation). Their use as social-control mechanisms can be labeled their *unintended but beneficial consequences* as social institutions.

Now let us consider the whole question of social control generally. Many social institutions are institutions of, among other things, social control. Education and schools, for example, instill moral precepts and examples that inhibit drives and desires that might otherwise be socially destructive. The layman least often appreciates to what extent religion and the family are mechanisms of social control. He tends to take these institutions at face value and not notice what we can call the dimension discovered by anthropological research. In effect, what anthropologists have come to believe can be summarized thus: men live in societies by necessity, not choice;

man is a social animal. Now, the only mechanical system which operates smoothly over a long period is one which has self-righting mechanisms to correct and adjust malfunctioning. Since human society consists as it does not of parts like cogs and levers which are subordinate to the whole machine, but of human beings, with needs, drives, desires, and quirks all their own, there are bound to arise clashes of interest and desire. Some people are stronger than others, some cleverer than others, some harder-working than others. In order that some do not crush others it is necessary that systems of ameliorating these clashes of difference and of desire be devised. These are the institutions of social control. We bring up our children in the family, in the church, and in the school, and we teach them ideas and standards which prevent them from tearing the society apart when they grow up—almost as if society, by encouraging education, is taking care of itself. This is called "socialization" and is perhaps the principal instrument of social control. There are, however, other instruments equally important. One is what measures we apply when people break the explicit rules of society, that is, the law; the other is the central control and giver of orders in the society, that is, government.

Take as an example the riots which occurred in successive summers in the United States. There were clear cases of the breakdown of a system of social control. Sometimes lawbreaking was involved (looting and violence) and one response was evoked (police); at other times additional response had to be brought in (troops). In the ordinary course of events lawbreakers are hunted down by the police and arrested for trial. The police, the courts, and the prisons are thus important mechanisms of social control, their roles being to punish, to reform, and to deter. When city authorities were unable to quell the riots, the state authorities called out the National Guard—reserve army units commanded within the separate states. When this was insufficient, as in Detroit in 1967, the

83

federal government ordered in the regular army. Thus governmental agencies are also agencies of social control. The government forces us to pay taxes; it drafts young men; it issues and withdraws passports; it imposes regulations on air safety, car safety, broadcasting; and so on. To a very large extent in our society that thing we call the government is the most visible mechanism of social control.

This is very different from the state of affairs among the Nuer, earlier discussed, where there are no policemen, courts, or even government. How do the Nuer manage to order and control their social life? The answer is, mainly through their kinship system of lineages. Among the Nuer, kinship is the principal mechanism of social control. In our society, kinship, if it ever was a principal mechanism, has long ceased to be important in economic, political, or religious matters; yet it still plays some role in the matter of social control. Our society is bigger, more complex, more differentiated than Nuer society. It would be impossible to regulate it on a kinship basis alone without radical alteration in such things as the profit motive, the idea of charity, equality before the law, the price mechanism, national identity, and so on. Before developing this point, however, let us consider the principal views that have been entertained on the question of the nature of social control in the history of anthropology.

One of the oldest views is the view that a society is like an organism which has a kind of self-regulating balance in it that should not be altered. In various forms, this theory is found in the writings of Plato and Aristotle and Confucius. In his major political work, *The Republic*, Plato is wrestling with the problem of explaining why he is living at a time of rapid and, he thinks, disastrous social change. He strives both to *explain* this change and to seek remedies for it. In his attempt, he discusses the idea of justice because that is what a good society should offer. Having dismissed various suggestions as to what justice is, he proceeds to outline a theory that says justice is each person doing what he is best-suited, naturally born, to do. A just state is one which ensures that men can act in accordance with their true natures. Once such a state exists how can decay and degeneration be prevented? By wise and just rule by wise and just rulers. These rulers must be of the highest maturity and caliber, utterly disinterested, and devoted to their task. Their rule must involve a very tightly controlled educational system which sees to it that those fit to rule are raised properly and everyone else is trained to do what he is suited to do. All straying from this just pattern must be stopped before it has begun; people and ideas must be closely watched.

Wondering whether any other political system would be as stable as the one he proposes, Plato considers the outcome of democracy. He argues that democracy, the rule of all, would feed the ambition of those who would grasp power. An oligarchy (a group of tyrants) would gain control. But then the same rivalries would develop between the tyrants, and one would seize supreme power and become dictator. The result of this would be plots by rivals and enemies which would either succeed or fail. If they succeeded there would be a new dictatorship and new plots; or a new oligarchy and the renewal of struggle for supremacy; or democracy and the rise of potential tyrants. If the plots should fail, they would revive at the dictator's death. Whatever the outcome, the whole cycle would start over. Stability *and* justice, Plato thought, could only be ensured in his perfect state.

Aristotle, who was something of a biologist, drew a comparison between society and the animal world, and pictured society as a collection of organs working together at their various jobs. This comparison was already embryonic in Plato, but Aristotle pushed it much further. His main problem was to modify what he regarded as Plato's somewhat extremist ideas, but he too seems to have sought stability as well as justice. This makes his modifications of Plato utterly

85

lose force in the face of the cogent and convincing arguments Plato deployed.

Confucius seems to have faced similar questions: the nature of good (stable and virtuous) government as a cure for endless uprising, war, and social change. He drew a different comparison—directly with the family itself picturing society as a huge family, and the government as the head of this family; good government was paternal government, good citizenship was filial piety. At least Confucius compared society with something also social—the family—not to a machine or an organism.

These early views of the need for social control see it not so much as a matter of harmonizing individual differences and conflicts, but more as a matter of tailoring, trimming, or coercing the individual into a predetermined mold. The rebellious slave, the person who does not want to be controlled by a patriarch must be suppressed and forced to fit in, or better, brainwashed so that all his disruptive tendencies are eliminated. The ideas of society as an organism or as a family have dangerous sides to them, because they are used not just as analogies to explain, but as ideals to be lived up to. Both analogies must have been very beguiling, because until very recently Plato and Aristotle in the West and Confucius in the East were revered as founts of social and political wisdom rather than as early explorers in a field we have learned much more about since, although doubtless not without their efforts.

In the seventeenth century in the West a rather new version of the nature of social control existed which abandoned the organic and family comparisons and substituted a comparison of people in society with the parties to a legal contract. Men came down from the trees, realized they were in danger of hurting and destroying each other, and instituted a contract, a mutually beneficial agreement to behave well, which they found the means to enforce.

86

The trouble with *all* these comparisons is that they broke down. The view that society was like an organism hardly matched the facts of social change or reform, and led to dangerous extensions such as labeling societies as old, young, mature, decadent, and so on, in analogy with the biological life cycle. These extensions are dangerous because they are oversimplified and misleading. They divert attention from the immediate problems of reforming and improving society, and encourage pointless and arbitrary quests for the correct labeling. Contract theory, too, was a bit naive. It hardly explained why there was so much upheaval and revolt in so many societies if they were based on contracts freely entered into. It ignored the element of coercion so prevalent in social control, and by necessity operated with the false notion that society began when the need for the contract was perceived and then duly instituted. Apart from the fact that if there were a beginning of society we know nothing about it since it clearly antedates written historical records (and archaeology notoriously tells us little or nothing about society), there remains the point that all the animals which we are most closely related to are social animals. Social life, then, preceded reflection on our social problems and certainly much preceded any such notions as contract or agreement.

The key question prompted by contract theory is, was there ever such a thing? Since man has always been a social animal, then the monkeys or their ancestors must have been the contractors. If this is absurd, how about a sophisticated refinement? Of course there never was any time or place when any actual contract was drawn up; society was not invented by someone somewhere for some reason. Instead one could say it was helpful to talk *as if* that were the case. The English common law, the United States constitution, were *in a sense* contractual bases for living in society. This revised view also has the advantage of suggesting that we—people—make up society and it is our continuing decisions to go on

THE STORY OF SOCIAL ANTHROPOLOGY

doing this that keeps the whole thing going. Thus we regain our lost importance as decision makers, even controllers.

Comparing society to a family is misleading too. A family has a head, there by legal ascription, not achievement. The senior male or female is the head of family in China. A family is a hierarchy, with the older persons having control over the younger. A society as we now envisage it need not be a hierarchy; indeed it can be the case that all men are equal. True, there is usually government and a head of state. But we like to think that being elected head for a short time is something a man must work hard for and deserve before he achieves it.

In addition to these theories the seventeenth century also saw society compared to a machine, in which people were cogwheels, institutions were bigger wheels, and the object of the whole thing was to run smoothly. In this respect the machine analogy is similar to the organic one. But as time went on the sinister overtones of regarding people as mere cogs in a machine began to get noticed and scored; yet when modern collectivist philosophies like fascism and communism appear they view mankind very much in these rather horrifying terms: cogs are relatively unimportant vis-à-vis the whole mechanism, and if one cog ceases to function, the thing to do is pull it out and replace it.

This reduction of the importance of individual people, with their hopes, aspirations and unique qualities, to cogs, had something to do with the plausibility of the metaphor in the first place. Role theory tends very much to see people as replaceable parts. It says that people in society play various roles, like the roles in a Shakespeare play. Each of us plays the roles of parent, friend, child, pupil, teacher, worshiper, and so on at different times of the day. Some roles are *ascribed* to us by the society (child, parent); others are *achieved* by our own efforts (hero, policeman, businessman). Most achieved roles, like the roles in a Shakespeare play. Each of us plays which a wide range of behavior is appropriate—but very closely defined—only a narrow range of behavior being appropriate—for example, the role of being king, or president, or secretary of defense, or archbishop of New York, or principal of a high school. It is also characteristic of these narrowly defined roles that they can be filled by only one person at a time (whereas the role of brother can be filled by any number of people at the same time) and when there is a vacancy it must and will be filled. People *replace* each other in these roles: the roles themselves go on. The society goes on, the individuals grow defective and die, hence the temptation of the cog-wheel analogy. Apart from the moral objections to comparing human beings to an organ or a cog, the fact remains that they are not simply organs or cogs. So far we have discussed social control as natural like an organism, social like a family, mechanical like a machine, and contractual or voluntary as in law. Two further theories remain to be considered: that social control should not be necessary at all (anarchism); and that it, or the lack of it, is part of the dynamics of social growth and development.

Rousseau is the father of the view that social control is something quite regrettable and unnecessary which we should aim to destroy.[4] In crude approximation (he modified his views later) his thesis was that men were naturally well-intentioned and cooperative; there was no true or natural conflict of interests between them. In the artificial world created by society, however, they somehow get all their natural instincts twisted and contorted, so that they end up mutually antagonistic and in perpetual competition. What Rousseau is saying is that man uncorrupted would not need social control; he would live in harmony. *Society* creates the situation where social control is necessary. The solution is to sweep away the conditions that are corrupting man and creating the necessity for social control. The way to do this is through education. By reforming

[4] Jean-Jacques Rousseau, *Emile*, 1762.

upbringing, by eliminating all corruption, man will throw off his social chains.

All this seems to me quite implausible, and in the discussion in the next chapter I shall try to indicate why I think that quite the reverse is true: namely, that human beings, because of their diversity and individuality, have widely differing interests which clash constantly, and that fundamentally society and social control are indispensible mechanisms for mediating and ameliorating these conflicts.

Let us consider once again the nineteenth-century ideas of evolutionism and social Darwinism. The problem-situation was this: What is the nature of social control, given that society is not like a human body, not like a patriarchal family, not like parties to a contract, not like a machine? How is it that, while human societies differ greatly in the means and their degree of social control, they all have some? The Nuer seem to have little, a dictatorship has a great deal, American society is somewhere in between. What was needed was a theory which related the amount of social control to the needs of the society. This was provided by applying the theory of evolution yet again. Social control is a mechanism which helps a society in the struggle for survival. Those societies where the struggle is not acute (the Nuer) can do with little social control; those where competition is fierce (Europe) need quite a lot. Is it not perhaps noticeable that in times of deep peril to the society, as during war, everyone accepts that much stricter social control is necessary than at other times? Just as most animals have in the course of evolution changed their bodies, their pelts, their diets to adjust to their surroundings, so human beings have changed their society the better to adapt to their environment. Among the devices involved is the amelioration of social conflict. A society which fails to deal adequately with internal social conflict weakens and possibly ultimately destroys itself. This is the message of evolutionism. Mechanisms of social control are directed toward ensuring a smoothly running society which can grow and prosper. Those not up to this fail to survive.

Much of today's thought about these matters has its line of descent from evolutionism. We are all evolutionists now, however watered-down our ideas may be from strict Darwinism. In the twentieth century, especially, there has been adopted the additional theory of functionalism. This assumes that since societies are refined mechanisms, each piece must have a definite function, or part to play, in the whole. So we are back to organisms and cogs. If there is violent social conflict, as among Corsicans, as in black America, then, unless it is sporadic, it must serve some purpose. One anthropologist has suggested that feuds among the Nuer serve to define and identify Nuer groupings against each other and against the outside world. Thus social conflicts are inherent, and social controls to keep them in bounds will always be necessary. It does not follow, however, that perfect civil peace and completely harmonious social living will result.

So theories of social control have progressed from one extreme to another until a sober midpoint has been reached. At the one extreme is Rousseau's view that social control is only necessary because man's nature has been ruined by society; at the other extreme is Hobbes's view that social control is necessary because man is a beast who would make his own life a misery without it. The middle course we steer nowadays is that while not all men are good, not all men are evil either. Control is thus necessary for those who are evil and those who are not sufficiently good.

The range of social controls is very great, but the most obvious of them, as we have mentioned before, are the police and the law. If we break the law in our society we are liable to be pursued by the police and brought before a court. Our knowledge that this can happen is certainly a control on our behavior. First of all, knowing that this is a possibility discourages us from breaking the law. Secondly, if we do break it, knowing what might happen, we try to conceal our misdeed, or our authorship of it. Thirdly, if we fail in all these we try to elude the police, unless stricken by pangs of conscience. Fourthly, if we fail in this, we plead not guilty in court. And finally, if we fail in our plea we appeal. The legal part of our system of social control appears to be very elaborate and powerful.

What would happen if there were no police, courts, laws, or anything? This might look like a hard question, but in fact we know the answer. Already we have considered the Nuer, who certainly lack police, even if they do not lack something like laws and something like courts—if we understand "laws" as rules which have serious consequences and if we understand "courts" as places where these serious consequences are discussed. If we take a stricter view of law as *written* rules and courts as formal institutions charged with dealing with infractions of written rules, then all preliterate societies, Nuer included, have no law and no courts. As I shall try to show, such a strict view, which looks hard-and-fast, is in fact more misleading than useful.

Let us consider now a people whose social organization is even simpler than that of the Nuer—not that the Nuer system is that simple—namely, the Bushmen. The Bushmen are a small-statured, yellowish-brown people who live by hunting and gathering plants in the Kalahari desert of southwest Africa. They are a very ancient people, probably the oldest inhabitants of Africa. They are very tough and good at surviving in the harsh conditions of the desert. They are especially skilled hunters and trackers in areas where game is hard to come by. They live in wandering groups, called bands, which number at various times between twenty and one hundred men, women, and children, who roam their part of the desert in pursuit of water and food. Several of these bands which are connected by kinship identify themselves as a tribe. Often in the dry season the band splits up and smaller groups go in different directions, to reunite when the rains come.

The Bushmen are remarkable in that they have no one among them who specializes in being a chief, no one who specializes in being a priest, and no tribal political authority of any kind. And yet, they live most orderly lives. They recognize murder and theft as crimes and punish them, and one does not find these crimes rife among them. This is re-markable, considering that they have no police and courts and even no written rules of any kind; there would seem to be no designated authority to administer punishment or correc-tion and to enforce rules. But the Bushmen are not saints; crimes do occur. And while there may be no written rules, all adult Bushmen know what is allowed to be done and what is not. How then do they cope; how are their unwritten rules enforced?

The answer is, in a way, simple and obvious. Such authority for disapproval and punishment, as may be appropriate, re-sides in the (males of the) band as a whole. The rules are enforced by the (males of the) group as a whole. If there is a murder, it is not difficult for such small groups to find out who did it. Every night when the sunset has prevented further hunting and gathering and the food has been eaten, the adult men gather round their fires and talk among themselves. If a crime has occurred they will discuss who did it and what should be done about him. When they reach an agreement, they act. Their severest punishment is to drive the delinquent out of the band. In the harsh conditions of the Kalahari desert this means almost certain death, unless the delinquent can find his way across the immense distances to another Bush-man band and persuade its members to let him join them.

93

For less serious breaches of the rules, less final forms of social disapproval are invoked.[5]

What lesson is to be drawn from this example? Are the Bushmen so very different from us? It would seem so, for there the whole adult group is involved in the interpretation as well as the laying down of the rules, and the whole adult male group discusses what shall be done, and then does what has been agreed to. How different from our society where the whole matter is in the hands of specialists in specialized institutions: legislators, lawyers, policemen, judges, jailers, and so on. Indeed, in our society, although authority and control flow from agreement by the group as a whole, small, well-organized pressure groups (like the temperance people) can get laws passed (prohibition) which deny the majority the pleasure they seek. In a consensus society like that of the Bushmen this is impossible. But is our society so very different? Are we not simply saying that the Bushmen are a more successfully democratic society than ours? Are we not simply saying that when, as in our society, democracy has to control huge areas and huge numbers of people, it is possible for carefully organized and well-planned campaigns to flout the will of the majority because of the indifference, inactivity, poor organization, or ignorance of the masses, all of which problems result from size and numbers? Democracy is unlikely to be perfect in any group too large for all members to know each other personally.

On what grounds do I say this? I say it because I am inclined to think that the situation in our society is not at all so radically different from Bushman society in the essential matters of making and enforcing rules. I think that our rules are made in theory by all of us, and are enforced in theory by all of us. I would concede that sometimes practice may differ

---

[5] A beautiful, non-technical evocation of Bushman life is to be found in two Laurens van der Post books, *The Lost World of the Kalahari*, Apollo, New York, 1963, and *The Heart of the Hunter*, Apollo, New York, 1966.

from theory, as in the case of prohibition, but I would contend that if such dislocation became systematic we would have a breakdown of law and order.

We have a notion in our society of the law coming into contempt. A very serious view is taken of this, and there is even a law which gives the courts very wide powers to deal with people who bring the law or the courts into contempt. Why should this be? If the law is brought into contempt, tha. is, if people's trust in the laws enacted and enforced in their name is undermined, the system breaks down. For example, lawyers already sense great dangers in the laws concerning parking and drugs. Parking laws are so drafted that even hyperrespectable citizens, who strive to their utmost to avoid brushes with the law, can find themselves either forced to violate the parking laws or violating them inadvertently (which is no defense). The laws on drugs are very severe, yet there are few people in high schools or universities who do not know where drugs can be purchased, from whom, which people have drugs and are therefore "in possession," and so on. If we fail to tell the police of this we are all criminal accomplices. Both parking and drug laws have failed to get us to endorse them wholeheartedly. We commit parking violations and we do not report on all the drug activity. We begin then to dislike policemen because they give us parking tickets, and we reinforce this dislike when we see them trying to hunt down what we consider relatively harmless experimentation with soft drugs. If we broaden drugs to include alcohol, and recall the minimum-age drinking rules of many states, then the extent to which we all conspire to thwart the law, and thus increasingly make its enforcement difficult, becomes clear. If, all of a sudden, everyone refused to pay his parking fines, refused to turn up in court, and so on, the entire system would indeed break down. If everyone suddenly stopped co-operating, what could be done? There are not enough police-men to make us do what we refuse to do. (In New York City

95

the degree of noncooperation got so bad at one point that the authorities declared an amnesty on unpaid traffic violation tickets, the point being that the task of following them all up and enforcing them was becoming mammoth.) In other words, the law works because there is a tacit agreement, a consensus on it, even if we delegate the specialized tasks like enforcement to specific individuals and institutions.

Thus we can perhaps see that the authority for such social control as is enforced by the law does indeed flow from the society as a whole. Or, to put it another way, some form of social control or social constraint is part of what we mean by a society. A society without rules, which means without controls, because a rule is something that can be broken, is not a society. Control is not *all* we mean by a society, of course. While anarchists, for example, believe that some form of organization of our behavior is necessary for social living, they agree with Rousseau that man left alone and uncorrupted would voluntarily impose upon himself all the controls necessary for harmonious social living. We might say that this opinion stems from a very simple view of human nature: that man is good and cooperative, not selfish and destructive. However, the theories of Sigmund Freud, who gave us psychoanalysis, are of some help here, for Freud read some anthropology (Frazer) and reflected on its problems. His ideas are by no means accepted in anthropology, but they have been very influential, especially in the United States.

Psychoanalysis claims that we are involved in tormented social relationships from birth, that there is no escape from these, and, moreover, that there is no personality formation without these essential human relationships. They are, of course, those of the immediate human family, especially relationships to and with father and mother. If we oversimplify a little we might say that Freud sees the child's relations with his parents, including his love of them, his secret hatred of them, and his identification with them, as essential phases of life to be gone through and experienced. Exactly what throws the development of these relationships off, so that distorted and sick personalities emerge, is not clear. What is clear is that human nature cannot be cleansed, or perfected. We all feel these things, and maturity consists largely in learning to cope with them. These phases, or something like them, are part of the process of learning about the world. To learn about the world is to learn that there is a reality out there which is harsh and unyielding while learning at the same time that there is a self which is identifiable, that is, different and some-how separate from the world out there.

Freud was extremely pessimistic about all this. He argues in his famous book *Civilization and Its Discontents* that living in a civilization itself involves distortions, guilts, and repressions over and above what all men have to suffer, and we cannot do away with the one without doing away with the other. Since we do not know how to live without either, and especially without a sense of reality or identity, they have become part of the human condition. Crudely, we cannot expect to build a society where no one will be mentally ill; rather, it seems that the more civilized we get, the worse will get our emotional conflicts, so that there will always be a need for psycho-analysis of those whose development goes wrong.

Completely opposed to the anarchist view that man left to himself and not corrupted will cooperate with his fellows and impose his own social controls is the view of what has come to be called totalitarianism. This is a view shared by extreme right- and left-wing political parties, to the effect that government central direction and control should be extended into every nook and cranny of the society, into every aspect of every individual's daily life. The most famous blueprint for this supercontrol is in *The Republic* of Plato. He there suggests the state must have complete control over education, the arts, marriage and the raising of children, and so on. His reason for all this is, as we have seen, that he wishes to arrest social change, which he fears is always for the worst. The only way to do this is to take all aspects of the society into the hands of those who will not allow this change to occur. These "guardians" need a lot of power, because if there is a gap in their control there is a possibility of ideas of change getting around. The most complete realization of Plato's blueprint, for not completely different reasons, is in Communist China. There the total control imposed by the government is justified by its fears of counterrevolution, in other words, regressive social change. Of course, it is not the same social change that Plato feared, namely the degeneration of the perfect state. Rather it is a regression toward the kind of society Plato approved of, but of which the Chinese Communists do not. More specifically China fears the return of capitalism and bourgeois democracy. Plato had nothing but contempt for trade and commerce, but he preferred democracy—bourgeois or otherwise—to tyranny by the Communist party or anyone else.

In China the state and its organs intervene in almost every conceivable aspect of life. Where, with whom, and how each person lives, moves, and has his being is completely under state control. The individual, as we call him in the West, is downgraded in importance, and the people are explicitly told that the individual is nothing, the state is everything. The revolution was not made for the people; people are made for the revolution. Revolution and struggle make for virtue, and virtue is to be sought by sinking oneself in the collective identity of the revolution and struggle, not by the cultivation of individual excellence and virtue.

Social control in our society is highly diversified with a long and complex history. Our official philosophy is that social control should be exercised by the state only to the minimum extent necessary; otherwise social control should be a matter for families and individuals to decide themselves. These limits on state intervention are considered people's rights: their rights to live and work where they please, their right to marry whom they please, their right to speak and think what they please, and so on. Our society has enshrined the principle that as broad a range of conduct as possible should be ignored by the state. The limits of this tolerated range can be illustrated by the following famous story. A man was arraigned before a magistrate and charged with assault and battery, namely punching another man in the nose. In his own defense the man said he had not punched the man, that he had simply been exercising his basic freedom to swing his arm about and the other fellow had simply put his nose in the way of the arm. The judge found the man guilty and admonished him as follows: "Your freedom to swing your fist is limited precisely by the location of your neighbor's nose."

Why do we have these social controls? The answers to this question again turn on views of human nature. These cover a spectrum. Just as Rousseau believed all men were good, Thomas Hobbes maintained that they were all selfish and greedy and could not be left to themselves. John Locke, while allowing that there are bad ones among us, believed that basically men were rational and thus capable of seeing their best interest and setting up the social controls of society for their own benefit. Aristotle too believed that men were rational. Plato was a real sociologist: clever as they were, he argued, men could not help but let their society drift into degeneration unless something radical in the way of control was done about it. In the Bible we find a curious view of human nature. The Old Testament constantly gives us a picture of the Israelites needing to be called back to the path of righteousness from their sloppy and indulgent yielding to false gods. Men are seen as good-willed, but weak, strongly open to temptation. What they need therefore is a set of very clear rules quite harshly enforced. Man's proneness to temptation and sin, indeed his original sin, leads to early Christianity endorsing the very strict social controls of the Middle Ages, the feudal subordination of serf to lord, of master to slave, and the strict watch for heresy and error in religious writing, worship, and belief.

All kinds of different justifications for imposing social controls have been offered at different times and places. Currently the most common view is that some of us are bad, some of us are weak, and all of us are thus in need of protection against ourselves and others. This is why centralized social control exists in our society. What, though, is the reason for parental social control, or school social control? Fundamentally we explain it today by the word socialization. Socialization is a subdivision of education. Usually we think of education as teaching some subject like mathematics or geography. But we can also look at it in the wider sense of teaching us how to live in the society to which we belong. We not only have to learn that children are not equal to adults; we have to learn what is known as good manners, correct behavior, and so on. We learn there are rules which govern or control or constrain our freedom of action. We are quite at liberty not to obey them; they are not effective controls in that sense, but we may choose to impose self-restraint on our own exercise of that liberty because we know the sanctions which are applied to those who break them. Just as we know the penalties the law prescribes for certain behavior—fines, going to jail—so we know that if we sass adults they will stop pocket money or smack us. If we violate good manners we may find we are chastised, sneered at, not invited to parties, stared at in restaurants, and perhaps even dropped by friends we would want to keep. Another part of our education is learning just how much we personally can get away with. The more amusing and striking of us can usually get away with a great deal more than the rest. Be that as it may, social control is not only externally imposed on us. Socializing in effect means learning the sort of behavior that is acceptable in the society, why it is that these standards are generally accepted, and how far we can get away with violating these standards, should we so desire. We will want to only to the extent that we do not understand those standards of behavior we endorse, or to the extent that we have reasons of our own for rejecting them. Any control then exercised over us is exercised by ourselves. If we can face all the consequences we are quite at liberty to reject all social control of any kind.

There is no reason, then, for us to bristle against social controls in general. However, in our society we do allow and even encourage *discussion* of social controls and action to reform them. Where the controls are centralized, as in the case of the law, this is straightforward. If enough people can be converted to the political party which wants to reform the law to elect it with a majority, then the reform has a good chance of becoming the law. What controls are more difficult to stomach are things like good manners, polite ways of speaking, habits of deference, and so on, which are not enjoined on us by the state by any means and which may strike us as totally unnecessary. How can we do anything about these? They can be changed, but change is slow and requires dedication. Once upon a time women could not smoke or drink in public, or go into bars. The way this was changed was that certain women decided to brave the sanctions and go ahead and do it. They were greatly aided by a general social upheaval caused by the First World War, when for the first time masses of quite respectable women went to work. Once women were seen at work, society became ready to accept their demands. Nevertheless, it was a hard battle and one which is still going on. Society, in other words, is a very strong and resilient object, and although it yields when it meets an irresistible force, it usually does so slowly and while exacting an enormous cost.

CHAPTER FOUR

The Nature of Society

WHAT sort of picture of society emerges from this discussion of the ideas of anthropologists about religion, the family, and the political, legal, and other mechanisms of social control? Is society a good thing or a bad thing? Or is it neither good nor bad but simply necessary? But if it is necessary, is every part of it equally necessary? Clearly not, is the lesson anthropology teaches above all. Whereas economists study their own and similar societies, as do sociologists and even political scientists, anthropologists systematically make it their job to look at a great many very different societies. Once this is done a new perspective is gained: the notions of good and bad and of necessary or unnecessary take on complications. Law and police seem necessary to us, but not to the Nuer or the Bushmen. We cannot easily say a custom is good or bad without a careful look at its role in the society. It is not even clear what is natural any more; the practices of Hausa mothers avoiding their babies and men avoiding their mothers-in-law come to seem quite natural after initial unfamiliarity.

So, in the end, what sort of a picture of society as a whole and its processes has emerged from this historical quest? To some extent this will involve reinvoking material already discussed, but from a different angle and for different purposes. The problem we are now concerned with arises in the following way.

Men discussed their society long before they became self-conscious and realized they were discussing something, and of course long before it occurred to them that sitting around discussing something or other could be given a name like sociology, anthropology, or physics. Or before study in general and the study of society in particular became social institutions themselves. For most of the history of mankind those who did discuss other societies looked on them as specimens—hardly to be compared with their own. This aloof, even disdainful attitude is apparent in Greek references to their "barbarian" neighbors, and even in references to slaves in the society of the Greeks themselves. This parochial attitude—"I know what I like, I like what I know, and what I know and like is best"—lasted well into the nineteenth century, and in its own way was only reinforced by the theory of evolution. This indeed provided a rationale, if one was required, for arrogant attitudes. It allowed Europeans to indulge in what was known as "wog bashing," secure in the conviction that such lesser breeds had to be made civilized if they were to progress. The great imperial mission of Britain was conceived in these terms, namely doing the world and the colonized peoples a favor by bringing them into contact with civilized government and mores with the hope that sooner or later they might become advanced enough to join civilization on equal terms. If the people who were being colonized resisted, force could be applied with a good conscience.

This attitude is so repellent, and it was so horrible to find its advocates appealing for support to science, particularly to the theory of evolution, that it is understandable that when the reaction against it came it was very violent indeed, and almost swept away the theory of evolution as applied to society. In the early years of this century the tables were completely turned in anthropology. Suddenly, anthropologists decided to go out and personally explore different societies, live intimately with their members and see what could be learned about them. It was not this exploration which led them to argue that savages were by no means as barbaric and inferior as they were sometimes made out to be. Their aim was to sweep out of anthropology the widespread prejudice against colored and primitive peoples. The American Indians had been decimated, West Africans enslaved, Tasmanian aboriginals wiped out, all with relative impunity because of such prejudice. And these attitudes had infected anthropology, which had catalogued "ye beastly devices of ye heathen," instead of telling the truth without distortion and prejudice, without arguing for the superiority of white society—the anthropologist's own society.

The "new" anthropology claimed that such unbiased truth-telling as now ensued was scientific and objective anthropology and that was why they commended it, but it is doubtful if this claim can be taken at face value. Theirs was primarily a moral quest. The quest was for an enlightened and just attitude to native people, to replace the oppression and injustice which were certainly rife. But detachment was never achieved. Anthropologists, rather, fell in love with the societies they studied. Their simplicity, their sanity, their humanity were often in stark contrast with the world the anthropologist left behind. Natives very often seemed to have come to terms with the human condition better than so-called civilized man. And so as a counterweight to images of savages dancing around inside the skin of sacrificial victims, anthropologists substituted what has been called the "wind-rustling-in-the-palm-trees" school of anthropology. But it is only fair to say that some anthropologists, especially Malinowski, perhaps the key figure in the sudden change in anthropology, managed to give us something nearer a recognizable picture of human beings living decent and sensible lives under very different circumstances and armed with very different beliefs and customs from ours. However, singing the praises of native society is no more balanced, unprejudiced, or truthful than is running it down as the lowest branch on the evolutionary tree. Reacting against the sins of their predecessors, today's anthropologists are in danger of romantically idealizing the natives they study.

In the 1920s we find anthropologists vigorously criticizing the oppressors and the unjust, that is, missionaries, businessmen, and colonial officials. In the case of missionaries, the havoc caused by well-intentioned missionaries as well as those less well-intentioned has been pointed out by anthropologists. Often cited is the effect the introduction of western tools can have on a simple society. Quite frequently such tools as the society already has are what one man makes. In other societies, however, intricate systems of specialization have grown up, where toolmaking is the province of a group which depends on tool exchange for a living. Sometimes, too, the price is high and the tool a mark of status, and occasionally tools have a semireligious significance. The simple charitable act by a missionary of making steel tools available to a native society, thereby instantly rendering obsolete their accumulated stock of tools, possibly also their whole group of specialists who make the primitive tools, their whole set of statuses connected with ownership of these tools, and also rendering meaningless all the rituals involving the manufacture and use of the earlier tools—the severe disruption of all this can be imagined. Clearly not all societies would suffer equally, but we know there are those which did suffer greatly in this way.

A documented example is the Yir Yiront of Australia. They used to have polished stone axes which played an important part in their economy and society. The stone for the axes was obtained by trading with other groups. They were male property, and while females were allowed to use them, they had to borrow them from their husbands or close male kin. The stone axe was a totem for one Yir Yiront clan. When well-disposed missionaries began to distribute short-handled steel axes, many of these relationships were upset. When women and young boys obtained axes of their own and no longer had to borrow from dominant males, "this led to a revolutionary confusion of sex, age and kinship roles. For the woman and boy the steel axe helped establish a new degree of freedom which they accepted readily as an escape from the unconscious stress of the old patterns—but they, too, were left confused and insecure. Ownership became less well defined with the result that stealing and trespassing were introduced into technology and conduct." The steel axes also confused the totemic system. "The steel axe, shifting hopelessly between one clan and the other, is not only replacing the stone axe physically, but is hacking at the supports of the entire cultural system."[1]

The same sort of critical points were made against missionary attacks on idols or prostitution; these things or practices frequently are deeply rooted in the social structure, and so in fighting them the missionary ends up saddled with the responsibility for massive changes in many aspects of native social life, changes he is not able or prepared to cope with. Missionaries were even known to pay converts. Businessmen exploited native labor. Colonial governments made massive blunders: they passed laws without regard to local custom and its rationale. They made boners such as thinking the golden stool of the Ashanti was a throne like any European throne and thus a symbol of power to be captured and sat upon. Sitting on the throne happened to constitute a monstrous desecration and insult to the Ashanti and started a wave of bloody wars—all because of a misunderstanding that a bit of sympathetic anthropology could easily have prevented. It

[1] Lawriston Sharp, "Steel Axes for Stone-Age Australians," *Human Organization*, vol. XI, 1952.

is difficult to say how many of these blunders were caused by sheer misinformation which anthropology could correct; sheer misinformation was, however, widespread.

Another danger awaited a newly alert anthropology intent on correcting misconceptions about other societies. This was a danger we have called relativism (see p. 39). Superiority is a vicious posture and set of attitudes; but it is not much nearer the truth to romanticize. The middle way between these extremes treats each society on its own merits and is purely matter-of-fact about differences between one society and another. But superiority has both a connotation in evolution (superior because higher up the evolutionary tree) and a moral connotation (superior because better, more civilized, more virtuous). Idealization has strong moral overtones too: the noble savage is better than we are. What are the moral overtones of the matter-of-fact view? Relativism is not merely the view that these strange native societies are as good as ours in every way, but that our standards of judgment of what is good and bad cannot be applied to them, because what seems good or bad to us may not seem good or bad to them. In cannibalistic societies killing and eating enemies is virtuous and heroic; in our society cannibalism is anathema. But, an anthropologist can argue, if you understand the cannibalistic society you will see that the problem is not that they cannot tell good from bad: they disagree with us about whether cannibalism is good or bad. They may not disagree with us about much; they, like us, may feel love and loyalty are good, stealing and infanticide are bad. How, then, can we say that they are wrong in approving cannibalism? We cannot cite the Bible; they do not accept its authority as a teacher of right and wrong. We cannot cite our laws, for they are not their laws. We can cite the so-called natural law—the moral truths that all men know in their hearts or consciences. But these cannibals plainly do not have it in their hearts to loathe and disapprove of cannibalism; on the contrary, they strongly approve of it. How then can we single out their cannibalism for condemnation, especially as it may play a vital role in their system of social ranking and control? Relativist answer: we cannot. It is not legitimate to apply *our* standards to *their* way of life. Each way of life has its own standards of good and evil, and they cannot be used to judge each other. All moral judgments are true only in their own cultural context and cannot be applied to people with different ideas.

This is relativism. It answers in a new way the question, "What is to be our moral posture toward these other societies we are exploring? Should we look on them as being as good as ours, or is there some other attitude available?" Anthropologists, on the whole, are relativists today. They believe that moral criticism can be made only in the context of a single society, and that for us to criticize the customs and practices of alien societies is arrogance.

Deeply as I sympathize with the anthropologists' rejection of superiority and idealization, I think that relativism is absurd. If I am traveling through the jungle with a colleague and he is killed by the natives while I escape, am I to say, like a good relativist, "Oh, it is merely the custom of the country to kill strangers"? True, deeper understanding may lead me to see that this custom came about because of the terrible things intruding strangers have done to these people. That, however, while it may make me more understanding, will not alter my moral judgment. A deeper understanding of a mugger may lead one to see that he behaves badly because of an unhappy childhood and keeping bad company. The fact remains that he behaved badly. Sympathetic understanding of another society does not at all mean we should approve or even condone all that goes on there. We must avoid being priggish or censorious, of course. But we do have moral ideas about how people should behave. Where these conflict we should try to come to a reasoned judgment, even if we agree to disagree.

Let us now discuss an attitude which I consider to be respectful yet critical, and neither arrogant nor smug. Then we shall go on to review our whole understanding of what sort of a thing society is, what we can do in and with it, and, especially, how it changes and gets better. This is an essential adjunct to our discussion of the attitude we take to the society of other peoples because those societies, now called underdeveloped, are increasingly becoming the world's main problems, and we need to clarify our notion of society in order to illuminate what those problems amount to and what sort of things can be done about them.

We have every right to make criticisms of other peoples, just as we have to make criticisms of ourselves. Our responsibility, in both cases, is to the people involved, namely, to criticize in a clear and reasoned way and with all due respect to the dignity of those whom we are criticizing. On occasion, our right to criticize is considered a way of improving ourselves, both morally and intellectually. To listen to what we are told, think about it, and try to criticize it is the way to learn. This is true in moral matters too: people present us with views and arguments from all sides on all issues all the time. It is slavish to listen to and accept any particular line; it is out of key with the spirit of our civilization. Now, since we adopt this attitude in our society, why should we not do it with others? There are various answers: because we become at worst arrogant, at best smug; because we fail to appreciate that other peoples are different, from a different way of life, culture, civilization, facing different problems. What right have we to criticize the Eskimo practice of abandoning old people? What do we know of the frightful hardships and struggle of Eskimo life? Do they not suffer enough that we should come along and make them feel guilty about an ancient and perhaps even humane practice? Is our criticism not just a lot of unsupported conclusions due to failure to understand?

This is a very plausible reply and we would not want to deny any of it for a moment. On the other hand, criticism is possible which is sympathetic, understanding, and perhaps even illuminating. It certainly does not presuppose the perfection of our own culture. We indulge in enough self-criticism to rebut that charge. And we learn from these other societies, too, about defects in ours. Nevertheless, it is possible that we might say to the Eskimo: This is a practice you might consider doing your utmost to eliminate. One way might be by limiting your families so that there is always food for old people; another might be to consider traveling to a less harsh climate where food is more plentiful either to settle or to leave old people. And so on. One does not expect the Eskimo to defend the practice as good in itself. But what if someone in another society does defend, say, a cruel practice like female infanticide, or headhunting? Then again, why not argue? Cannot one try to evoke sympathy for the helpless babe, perhaps even suggest the institution of adoption for someone who wants a girl, or special institutions for those malformed? Cannot one defend the prohibition of headhunting by indicating that a state of society is possible in which practically all threats to life are eliminated and that headhunting is inimical to this because if you hunt *them* they will hunt *you*? To stop it everyone has to stop it. If the status system is tied in with headhunting, or the concept of masculinity or warrior or whatever, one can argue that these honors can be awarded for other sorts of things. People may like their old ways, but they can also be convinced that they are better dropped if the rewards, such as a more secure existence, are great enough. The main tack to take is to try to find an inconsistency between two values in the society and to indicate that one value can be enhanced only at the expense of the other.

An example of this happening on a very broad front has

been outlined by E. Gellner.[2] He points out that wherever the chance arises, people all over the world have seized on industrialization as something they want, despite its Western character, and are prepared to go to great lengths and make extensive compromises to get it. This is very intriguing to industrialized societies, but it is no reason for them to be smug. Great inventions, such as the wheel, explosives, industrialization, wherever they originated, belong to all of mankind. It would be absurd of people to refuse to take advantage of the benefits such a thing conferred just because their nation or culture did not invent it. This way lies the madness of Nazi condemnation of Einstein's work as "Jewish science." For non-Westerners to spurn things they want because they are Western is a form of snobbery, if not of racialism. For Westerners to refrain from criticizing and discussing the moral and scientific ideas of non-Westerners is an inverted snobbery. It says, "You are as good as we and we do not criticize those we admire." And of course this is nonsense too. It is only those we admire and respect whom we really bother to criticize; others we dismiss out of hand. Indeed, to enter into critical discussion of a serious kind with another person is the true way of declaring that you take him to be your equal. His acceptance is a reciprocation. Not to do so is condescension or self-abasement, and both are foolish.

So, despite the dangers of our blundering and hurting feelings, it seems to me that if we are to learn from studying other societies we must be prepared to discuss them critically, including the quality of life they embody, the knowledge and moral ideas they have discovered.

Society is not a machine or an organism. There may be resemblances or analogies, but it is clear that the social world is *sui generis*, not governed by the laws of mechanics or the laws of growth and evolution. The decisive difference would

[2] E. Gellner, *Thought and Change*, Univesity of Chicago Press, 1965.

seem to be this: whatever laws there are in the social field are in some sense or other created by man or are the outcome of what men do. By contrast, the laws of mechanics and of biology are the laws that govern or control machines and organisms. Living organisms have the property of creating organizations: plant communities, schools of fish, ant nests, and so on. These communities behave in fairly regular ways and to a certain extent can be subsumed under the laws of biology. However, a strong difference develops when we look at organization among the animals, especially the higher animals. There we come across quirks of organization and behavior which could just as well be different and yet make no appreciable difference in the matter of survival. So why do such patterns as pecking order, the distribution of females between males, the development of leadership patterns, and so on develop? Of late, researchers in primate and animal behavior have been able to argue that some of these patterns can be seen to have biological survival value in the overall evolutionary scheme; but they do not deny that alternative patterns of organization might have equal survival value.

The same sort of consideration applies very much to human society. Man must live in society if he is even to survive, not to mention be rich and comfortable. Man needs to mate, and he needs to stick around to feed and bring up his children, because they are quite unable to fend for themselves for several years, and remain relatively weak for several years thereafter. But whether men live in large groups or small, with chiefs or without, practice monogamy or polygamy, hunt or cultivate, let men work and women laze, or vice versa, or neither, does not seem to affect survival. Societies displaying all these different organizational patterns in differing combinations exist. —

However, one general pattern seems to make a great difference, not to survival, but to success and wealth. This is the pattern of dividing the tasks. One man can kill or grow enough food for several if he puts all his energies into it. This practice allows the others to concentrate on other things, such as making weapons and tools, constructing dwellings, and so on. This lesson was taught to us by the great economist and philosopher Adam Smith. He wrote the first book in economics, *An Inquiry into the Nature and Causes of the Wealth of Nations* (1776.) He set out to discuss the problem of why some nations are wealthy and some are not, and how to make a nation more wealthy than it is. He developed the theory of the *division of labor:* if men specialize intelligently, they can manage to do more than if they all do all their own tasks. This may seem paradoxical: if you have ten men working ten hours, surely it does not make any difference whether each does his own job in all matters, or whether each one specializes. But it does. And the explanation is the basic fact of differences of human skills. Some men are excellent hunters but poor toolmakers: others are fine gardeners but hopeless cooks. And so on. It follows that hunting should be the full-time occupation of those good at it, while those not good at it should do something that suits their talents. That way the hunters will kill enough and perhaps more than enough for everyone, and the toolmakers will make many excellent tools and weapons, and so on. So effective is this system, argues Smith, that very soon the society is able, given certain conditions, to build up a surplus of goods. Now they may find that neighboring peoples, who have an abundance of salt, for example, have no good toolmakers, and are happy to swap their salt for tools. It may even be the case, salt being so precious and hard to find, that the people living near salt do very little else than package it for sale to their neighbors for food, and so on. Not only are people different in their talents—and specialization comes that way—but also different areas of the world are differently endowed—and specialization comes about that way also. The salt area may have no decent soil or game at all—all the more reason for swapping salt for food.

113

This buildup of surplus by specialization is very important. A man who looks after only himself is very vulnerable. He may fall sick and die because he cannot hunt or cook. If weather is bad, he may die because he cannot get enough food. Whereas, if by cooperation and specialization he has built up a surplus, he may ride out these periods of misfortune and still survive.

What we have learned so far is that it is in man's best interests to live in a society and become highly interdependent on other members of the society; not only is his survival better ensured, but so also is the growth of his wealth. This universal desire for wealth and leisure may explain the readiness, indeed eagerness, with which so many underdeveloped countries embrace the industrialization gospel of the West. However, society is not exhausted by its economic aspects; there is, for example, government.

Basically, Smith argued that the best thing governments can do is to leave things alone. They can enforce laws of honesty and so on, but the less they interfere with the economy, the more the wealth of mankind will grow. If, for example, the government puts a tariff on cheap salt from abroad it is forcing the consumer to pay more of his income for salt than he otherwise would need to, and he is thus poorer than he needs to be. Smith, in other words, pictures the economy as a vast and complex system of interrelationships which takes account of all the different talents and capacities of men, all the spread of natural resources from place to place, and in the marketplace brings one into contact with the other to their mutual advantage. This is a very beautiful theory, so striking that Smith himself was inclined to say it was almost as if there were a divine and benevolent plan behind it all, ensuring that if we each pursue our own best interest, we all benefit maximally. He called this providential aspect the "Hidden Hand" guiding us.

However, in this society of ours some men get very rich while others stay poor. Does a man with no talent, no resources, and no luck have to be condemned to being at the bottom of the heap of society? In a certain sense yes. But, we argue today, not all the way. The society is rich enough to afford to give such people at least a decent standard of living and way of life. If this is done we are interfering with the Hidden Hand and perhaps not getting the maximum benefit from specialization. True enough, but we are rich enough to forego being super-super-rich, at the expense of those at the bottom of the pyramid. The only way we can do this, however, is by intervening in the market and controlling the mechanisms so that the bottom people are not crushed. This intervention can be done in a piecemeal way by charities and benevolent firms; but not all victims are saved in this way, and so, inevitably, the government is brought in.

In the United Kingdom the question of the poor was debated throughout the nineteenth century under the rubric, the "poor law." The discussion turned on the question, what to do about the poor? Those who thought the poor had no one to blame but themselves (that is, they were poor because they were idle or unenterprising or poorly endowed) wanted the poor put to work. Those that saw poverty as partly a product of the system, of being feeble, of being sick, of being young, of just being unfortunate, wanted society to take care of them to a minimum decent level. The first group argued that this would encourage idleness and ruin the economy. The second group responded that it was a matter of human decency. Many of the pros and cons appear in some of Dickens's novels.

The idea that only the state is foresightful enough to run things for the benefit of everyone was precisely what Smith's theory had been an attack on. He had been criticizing mercantilism, which was a doctrine that state intervention in the economy was for the good of all. Now the poor-law question, the whole problem of injustice and suffering in society, led people to believe that only intervention by the state could ameliorate these ills. Others concluded that the society was so bad the ills could be wiped out only if the society itself were wiped out and rebuilt rationally and morally. A less extreme position than the latter was the view that if unbridled free enterprise led to suffering which had to be rectified by the state, was it not better to let the state control things from the start and see that no injustice ever began?

While in theory the idea that we can control, direct, and rationalize society is very appealing and even flattering, it is wildly impractical. A large modern society is so complicated, diverse, and intricate that no one person or institution can even get a complete overview, never mind start to direct its progress as a whole. This is a limitation many people refuse to recognize. The suffering is real enough; so is the fact that the society causes it. What is to stop us trying to rearrange the society so that the suffering does not arise?

In the first place there is the inability of anyone to achieve sufficient knowledge to have an overview of the whole society and so devise a proper plan. Then there is the more serious matter that it is difficult to predict what will happen as a consequence of your actions. What you want may indeed come about, but other things you by no means want may also come about. This is a serious matter, because to a certain extent human beings are unpredictable in their reactions and they may act so as to vitiate or cancel out any gains that may be achieved by your success. Action to alleviate poverty may result in undermining the incentive to work and thus the whole prosperity on which the attempt to alleviate poverty is predicated. Recognition of this sort of difficulty convinces some social scientists that we have to be slow, patient, and measured in our attitude toward intervention. Others take the view that only total intervention and total control will wipe out all suffering. What sociology and anthropology teach us is not a political lesson but a practical lesson, namely that however strenuous is the attempt to sweep away the past and replace it, all that is ever touched is only a small part of the myriad roles and institutions of which the society is constituted.

All this has been discussed by F. A. Hayek.[3] His view is that while free institutions and a free economy are riddled with faults and difficulties, they are nevertheless far and away the best framework in which human resourcefulness, inventiveness, and knowledge can be made maximum use of for the benefit of mankind. He indicates that planning a society is almost a contradiction in terms since it requires a knowledge no one can have, and it tries to leave unplanned areas for spontaneous change and growth. These latter are the most important factors in society, but they certainly cannot be planned: *that* is a contradiction in terms. Hayek tries to show us how society is a great human invention, but, unlike a machine or an organism, it is *the result of human action but not of human design.* Society is huge, untidy, amorphous— not to say invisible.

To a very considerable extent society is in the mind. That is, the ideas people have of the society they are living in affect very deeply the actions they take; and the actions they take, the way they play their roles, constitute, in a certain sense, the society they see in their minds. This sounds very complicated, but it is really very simple. If, when going to a government office, you believe these are people of great power and efficiency governed by strict sets of rules which they know by heart, you may well be timorous in your approach and downcast when told your request is against the rules. Your timorousness and downcastness in their turn influence other people's attitudes toward you, including the officials, who begin to believe it themselves. On the other hand, it is notorious that if you refuse to be diverted from your purpose, and you breeze around with the utmost confidence, you may get what you want despite the rule. In Hong Kong there is a very interesting

[3] F. A. Hayek, *Studies in Philosophy, Politics and Economics,* University of Chicago Press, Chicago, 1967.

case which reveals the problem of corruption of the civil service and especially of minor officials.

Chinese believe that they cannot get things from officials without oiling the machinery with a bribe. Thus, when they go to receive their much-prized British passport after naturalization, and are told by the counter clerk that there will be a small fee, they are not surprised and they pay up. Now there is no fee, but bribery is reinforced by the public's expectation and the official's venality. This is a microcosm of the whole problem of bribery in Hong Kong. Even incorrupt officials explaining a genuine and unexpeditable delay may have bribes thrust upon them, because it is assumed that the delay can be expedited that way. The poorly paid official who spurns the bribes and stands by the integrity of the service, even when all his fellows are taking it, has to be strong.

Now the belief in bribery stems from past times when it *was* part of the system, and acknowledged to be so. Why was it continued into the present? Of course, it must continue to work. That is, the shrewd Chinese would not pay bribes were it doing no good, and indeed in general they have stopped doing it to higher-level government officials where not only will it be spurned, but those proffering it may be prosecuted.

We see then a case where an institution (bribery) is sustained partly because the public believes in it, partly because the officials are venal, and partly because, since the officials can be bribed, when they have a choice of priorities it is relatively simple and straightforward for them to act according to the bribes they get. Officials are constantly in positions where they can deal with less urgent matters in any order they please and this is the sort of place in the system where a bribe might be effective. Now, of course, strenuous efforts can be made to close this loophole, for example, by date-stamping all files on delivery and insisting that they be dealt with in order. But there are so many urgent cases, so many misplaced documents, so many ruses, that the job is impossible. What then happens? The government fires officials and tries to clean up the surface. It raises salaries, but never enough. It tries to inculcate integrity and makes dismissal a penalty. It all helps a little, but still the bribe system works. In the end everyone comes to realize that the public's belief in it has much to do with its sustenance. People want things, and they really are convinced that a dollar in the right places will get them what they want. If they did not offer the "small fee," but asked immediately to see the superior officer to ask why the passport was not ready, they might find things a little different. But then again beliefs are important. Chinese in Hong Kong are a little afraid of the civil service: they feel that it pushes them around and that if they make a fuss things will go badly for them. What they do not realize is that this is true until substantial numbers are firm and confident with the officials and refuse to pay, and then the whole machinery of officialdom becomes much more amenable.

The foreign visitor to England, and indeed Europe in general, is struck by the patience with which everyone stands and waits in queues at bus stops, in offices, in stores, movie houses, and so on. In other parts of the world people push and shove and tell those serving the queue to hurry up. Sometimes queues are inevitable; but other times people are overdocile. If the public were vociferous enough about post-office queues, about traffic-jam queues, and so on, something would be done about it. As it is they accept it resignedly as part of the inescapable travail of living, and those who could ameliorate the queues go on requiring them.

We are dealing here with a very interesting matter, sometimes called the social perception of reality. Society and its institutions are very much of a reality in the way they impinge on us in our daily lives, all the time and in countless ways. And yet, in a crucial sense society is only as real as our continuing belief in it. The usual name for something which is there only because we believe in it is an illusion or a mirage. Can we conclude that it is an illusion that educates us, an illusion that drafts us into the army, an illusion that pays our salaries, and so on? Well, of course, money *is* partly an illusion. Most money in our society is no more than an entry on a pay slip, an entry in a bank ledger, and various signed checks. All this is obscurely related to the fact the people value gold. But why do they do so? After all, gold is just a yellow metal—who needs it? With or without reason people want it, so above all money is an illusion sustained by *us*.

So at the very least society is something halfway between illusion and reality. If the members of the society decide in large numbers not to believe in something, that something very soon experiences acute difficulties in operating. It is well known that if a large number of citizens decide to defy a law, that law becomes unenforceable. This has been the case with Puritan laws against festivals, such as Christmas, laws which are still on the books in England. It was true of the prohibition era in the United States, when defiance of the anti-drink laws led huge sums of money to fall into the hands of purveyors, and those criminal purveyors became heroes. Today, it seems as though certain drugs are in such widespread use that the attempt to enforce the laws against them is gradually stirring up more and more trouble, so that sooner or later the law will have to be changed because it is unenforceable—you cannot put a whole generation in jail. However, if the years it took for people to find out that prohibition was impracticable are any guide, the drug laws can be expected to stand for some time.

In short, social life is something we create among us, but which goes beyond us and therefore is not directly subject to our will. If we want to change things, we have to get enough people on our side to do so. When after the Detroit riots President Johnson said that whatever the measures that were taken to help blacks, fundamentally a change of heart would have to accompany them, he hit the nail on the head. The government can give people the incentive to change their hearts, and can help the blacks to live better and less un-happily. But in the end people's ideas are what count. If the hearts of men suddenly changed and they decided they would no longer discriminate, that would be the end of it: discrimina-tion would disappear.

What happens in anthropology? We start out with some curiosity about strange alien societies, usually primitive ones. We then find out that what they do and the way they do it makes perfectly good sense once we see the situation they are in and the way they see that situation. It makes such good sense that we are hard put to remember that some of their ideas are open to question. They may believe in magic, or they may practice human sacrifice. However much we understand their situation, and however well we grasp how they see it, we cannot forget that *we* think magic is false, and that human sacrifice is wicked. Thinking as we do, we have every right and even duty to air these matters if the opportunity arises, as when we are writing about the society or when a member of the society asks for our opinion. Of course, we may at the same time come to doubt the wisdom of beliefs and practices in our own society: we may wonder why whom you can marry should vary from state to state; why we take off our hats but not our shoes when we enter a home; why we reply to "How are you?" with "How are you?"; why we keep sex, but not violence or cruelty, out of children's movies and tele-vision; why we have attitudes of disgust or shame toward the body and its natural functions; why we knock on wood, avoid walking under ladders, or crossing the path of a black cat; why it is a greeting to clasp hands and shake them; and so on. Our coming to wonder at our own ways, no longer taking them for granted, is anthropological feedback, one of the most interesting consequences of exposing ourselves to other societies and ways of life.

Anthropology is the quest for knowledge about man and his social life. Knowledge is to be gained by asking questions, trying to answer them, then criticizing and improving the answers. The criticism of the answers we can make when we become anthropologists is so deep that we sometimes find ourselves criticizing the questions themselves too. We may begin by asking how can societies like the Bushmen operate with so little social control, and in the course of answering this turn the question back and say why on earth when the Bushmen need so little do we need so much in the way of mechanisms of social control?

This in turn leads us on into the whole question of the nature of society. In anthropology we start out not only taking our own society for granted, but taking the notion of society itself for granted. We think we know what society is. But increasing acquaintance with the myriad diversities and differences the human imagination has thrown up in the way of social institutions, moral ideas, and attempts at knowledge and explanation makes us come to doubt not only that we can take our own society for granted, but, as explained in this chapter, that we can take the idea of society itself for granted. Society, it transpires, is a very complicated and even nebulous entity. It resembles a brick wall in that if you run headlong into it you may get just as severe a hurt as from a brick wall (try running a red light or resisting arrest). It also resembles a mirage or a dream in that if enough people decide it does not exist, suddenly it will not be there. It exists in a third world, neither the world of physical objects nor the world of mental entities and thoughts, but a world where thought becomes action, action is within a framework of roles, and roles connect into institutions. This world, which perhaps also contains things like knowledge and mathematics, constitutes the social framework within which human life is lived, and conditions to a considerable extent what we can make of ourselves. It is therefore of the utmost interest that we explore and map it and that we are fully aware of both the extent and the limitations on our attempts to reform and improve it.

For Further Reading

IN addition to books mentioned in the footnotes, the interested reader might consult the following.

For a charming introduction to anthropology, Raymond Firth, *Human Types* (New York: Mentor, 1956) or E. E. Evans-Pritchard, *Social Anthropology* (Glencoe, Illinois: Free Press, 1964).

To get more detail on the history of anthropology, read Abram Kardiner and Edward Prebble, *They Studied Man* (New York: Mentor, 1963), which devotes a chapter to each of several key figures in the history of anthropology.

A moving nontechnical study of the contact of two cultures is Alan Moorhead's *The Fatal Impact* (New York: Harper & Row, 1966), the story of Captain Cook's voyages and their impact on Tahiti.

Nine Dayak Nights by W. R. Geddes (New York: Oxford University Press, 1961) is an exemplary portrait of a fascinating society and its folk tales by a contemporary anthropologist.

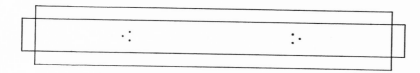

Glossary

Amazons: Ancient, legendary nation of female warriors said to have cut or burned off the right breast in order to use the bow better. They reproduced by means of annual visits to the Gargareans. The male offspring was either killed or returned to his father, the females were raised in the arts of agriculture, hunting, and war.

Americans: Numerous nation of farmers and industrial workers inhabiting a huge slice of the Western Hemisphere which extends from the temperate to the semi-tropical zone. The population is largely caucasoid, but 10 percent are of negroid and mixed stock. The main religions are Christianity and Judaism. Nuclear families live in separate residences located conveniently for the head of the family's job; no wider kinship grouping is recognized. Kinship is cognatic (that is, traced through either sex link). The government is a complexly layered political system, with branches at the city, county, state and national level.

Ancient Egyptians: Cultivators of the Nile Valley. They almost certainly had a bilateral kinship system, and were ruled over by a hereditary pharaoh. Ancient Egyptians had one of the earliest civilizations, with hieroglyphic writing. They

were chaotically polytheistic idolators and were notable for
their mummification of, and pyramids for, the dead.

Ancient Greeks: Aryan farmers, pastoralists, and merchants of
certain Mediterranean islands and the Greek mainland,
ruled by hereditary kings in council. Their kinship was
patrilineal but with the extended family household as the
unit of importance. They believed in a pantheon of gods
presided over by Zeus and the members of his family.

Anglo-Saxons: Pagan farmers and pastoralists who inhabited
England prior to the Norman conquest in a union of various
kingdoms under Alfred the Great. Cognatic kinship.

Ashanti: Matrilineal negroid agriculturalists of Southern Ghana.
Their several states are united into a confederacy ruled over
by a king, the Ashanti-Hene, whose symbol of office was the
golden stool. They believe in a great spirit who created all
things, and who manifests his power through a pantheon
of gods. Below these gods are first the lesser spirits who
animate trees, animals, or charms, and then the spirits of
the ancestors.

Australian Aborigines: Slim, brown-skinned hunters and
gatherers of the Australian subcontinent whose religion is
totemic. They wander in small patrilineal clans which
usually consist of a senior man and all his living male
descendants, their wives and children. The kinship system
pervades and controls all aspects of the social organization;
it is bilineal. There are no chiefs.

Azande: Negroid hunters, gatherers, and cultivators who inhabit the savannah of the Nile-Congo border. Organized into
several kingdoms, each is dominated by an aristocratic class;
their patrilineal kinship system does not correspond to
residence patterns. Their religious system, indeed their
entire way of life, is dominated by belief in witchcraft,
oracles, and magic.

British: Inhabitants of a temperate island off the northwest
coast of Europe. The population is largely caucasoid with

10 percent being negroid immigrants. They are generally Christians and are basically industrial. Some inhabitants engage in agriculture. Kinship and residence patterns resemble those of the *Americans.* Their political and legal system is unified and centralized. Their counties, parishes, and towns have only narrow areas of responsibility.

Bushmen: Small-statured, brown-skinned hunters and gatherers of South Africa, with a nonunilineal kinship system and a wandering pattern of residence, in small bands of around forty persons. Worship of the heavenly bodies and especially of the moon is widespread. They worship the rain, and possibly a supreme spirit.

Chinese: Numerous, mongoloid, peasant society inhabiting much of the mainland of East Asia, which extends from the zone of continental to that of tropical climate. It is one of the oldest civilizations and was literate long before the West. Extended families live in separate houses in agnatic (agnates: relatives in the male line) lineage villages. In imperial times, the government, which was centralized and bureaucratic, was operated by officials chosen by competitive examination. Their religious beliefs were syncretic (fused from several distinct traditions and embraced many kinds of gods and spirits, and was much overlaid by Buddhism, which spread from India.

Congo Pygmies: Small-statured hunters and gatherers of the dense forest areas of equatorial Africa, who trade their spoils for agricultural produce grown by their negroid neighbors. Organized into small bands of not much more than family size, they have no lineages. The principal object of their religious attentions is the forest itself, which provides them with home and livelihood.

Creek Indians: Matrilineal Red Indians of Alabama and Georgia. They were horticulturists, whose village organization was ruled by hereditary chiefs and elaborately recruited councils. They believed in a supreme being who lived in the sky and a host of lesser spirits in wind and animals. At the unique Green Corn Dance every wrong short of murder was forgiven.

Dakota (Sioux): Plains Red Indians, hunters in the past of buffalo and other game. They were tribally organized under chiefs and strongly patrilineal.

Desert Arabs (Bedouins): Nomadic, camel-herding Semites of the Arabian deserts. Strongly patrilineal, they are fierce, independent warriors who roam around in semiautonomous bands. Their religion is Islamic.

Filipinos: An ethnically and linguistically mixed people inhabiting a large collection of islands in the western Pacific. They range from primitive tribal people who are pagan to sophisticated town dwellers who are Christian or Muslim. Their kinship is everywhere bilateral; some tribes have hereditary chiefs, but overall the country is governed through modern Western-style democratic institutions.

Fox: Prairie Red Indian tribe of Wisconsin who were horticulturists. With bilateral social organization, they also had village councils with a chosen chief, and religiously inspired war-party leaders.

Gauls: Collective name for the Aquitani, Celts, and Belgae who inhabited the area of the Roman Empire bounded by the Alps, the Mediterranean, the Pyrenees, the Atlantic, and the Rhine. Little is known of their social organization.

Hausa: Negroid agricultural people of northern Nigeria, notable for their well-developed property concepts. Their kinship system is cognatic rather than unilineal, and they are organized as states under hereditary rulers. They are mainly Muslims.

Indians: Aryan peasants of the south-Asian subcontinent, comprising an array of tribes and peoples showing almost every conceivable social, political, kinship, and religious pattern.

Iroquois: Eastern Red Indians inhabiting northern New York State. They were agriculturalists and fishermen, who dwelled in long-house towns. Matrilineal, tribal, and ruled by chiefs, they were remarkable for banding their warring factions into a league of six nations. They believed in a great spirit and a host of lesser spirits and in the immortality of the soul.

Jews: General name for the Semitic herdsmen and agriculturalists who inhabited Palestine from early times. Tribally organized under patriarchs, they combined the doctrines of one god (Yahweh) and of being his chosen people into Judaism. A running dispute with the Roman Empire led to their defeat in A.D. 135 and the extinction of political nationality. Jews then dispersed throughout the Mediterranean and Europe seeking livelihood.

Manus: Melanesian fishermen and traders. Primarily patrilineal, without hereditary chiefs, they inhabit the Admiralty island of the same name off the northeast coast of New Guinea. They are ancestor-worshipers.

Masai: Tall, formidable negroid transhumant cattle herders of the grassland of Kenya and Tanganyika. Their kinship is patrilineal and organized into a rigid seniority and age-set system for males.

Mende: Negroid, patrilineal farmers and fishermen of Sierra Leone who form powerful secret societies from which chiefs and leaders are drawn. Christianity and Islam are widespread among them.

Nandi: Culturally similar to the *Masai,* the Nandi inhabit Kenya, but add sheep, goats, and agriculture to their means of livelihood. Patrilineality is cut across, as in the *Masai,* by age-set organization.

Navaho: Red Indians of the southeastern United States whose society was agricultural, matrilineal, and organized into bands consisting of several extended families, which ranged from one hundred to several hundred persons. Each band had a chief who achieved office through leadership. Elaborate religious beliefs involved the creator of man, Changing

Woman and her husband, the Sun, and a host of lesser spirits, including those of animals. They had an intense fear of ghosts and believed very strongly in witchcraft and sorcery.

Nuer: Tall, negroid, naked herdsmen who dwell in the savannah grasses and swamps of the tropical plains of southern Sudan. The kinship system is coextensive with the political, legal, and residence system. There are no chiefs. Men are organized and controlled through the obligations and rights of the agnatic kinship system and its lineages. Their religious system is complex with many kinds of gods and spirits, including a supreme being, *kwoth.*

Persians: Inhabitants of the ancient Aryan kingdom of Asia Minor which was based on the agriculturally rich Fertile Crescent, thought to be the cradle of all civilization. They worshipped many gods and regarded fire and cows as sacred. Their religion was overlaid with Zoroastrianism and Islam. Their society was probably patrilineal and was an absolute hereditary monarchy.

Romans: Aryan agriculturalists of the city-state of Rome in central Italy, which came to dominate first Latium, then Italy, and finally an extensive empire in Europe and the Mediterranean. Strictly patrilineal, the father of the family had absolute power over his children and wife; for a period, sons could own no property while their father was alive. Their government evolved in complex ways, from kingdom, to republic, to empire, sometimes democratic, sometimes despotic; and their religious system was eclectic polytheistic. Several later emperors had themselves proclaimed living gods.

Singhalese: Peasant and commercial farmers who make up the bulk of the population of Ceylon, a large island off the southern tip of India. They are Buddhist.

Tasmanians: Hunters and gatherers, moving about in small bands of kinsmen, without hereditary chiefs or government.

Each band had its own territory, to be interfered with at risk of war. They were akin to the Melanesian stock, polygamous and probably the original inhabitants of Australia. They were driven south by the arrival of the Australian aborigines from the north, and exterminated by disease and atrocity in the nineteenth century.

Trobrianders: Farmers of the Melanesian race who inhabit tropical islands off the northeast coast of New Guinea. Their kinship is matrilineal with chiefs; their religious system is pantheistic.

Yir-Yiront: Small tribe of aboriginal hunters and gatherers who inhabit the Cape York Peninsula of Australia. They have a patrilineal kinship system divided into the three lines corresponding to those with whom a man may not marry, those with whom it is preferred he marry, and those with whom it is preferred his sister marry. The patrilineal clans are also the organizational basis for the totemic religion. Their counting system does not go beyond 2; after that words like "a few," "several," and "many" are used.

This excellent historical introduction to the field of anthropology shows the important and fascinating connections between the study of primitive peoples and the reflections of philosophers on the nature of society and the social order. Throughout, Dr. Jarvie draws his illustrations of anthropological concepts and ideas from phenomena familiar to us in our own society.

The book concentrates on three main areas of society, and the connections among them. They are religion and magic, family and kinship, and social control. Religion and magic—essentially precursors to modern science and technology—are seen as man's attempts to understand and control his life and surroundings. Family and kinship are the most widespread means of organizing the groups necessary for social life: the group that reproduces and cares for children, and the group that procures food and shelter. Both belief systems and kinship systems are regarded as inputs to social control, which is partly internal (children are taught how to behave), and partly external (behavior is sanctioned and this gives power to certain men). Control is necessary because man lives in a hostile environment and must organize to survive. In small groups, organization can be spontaneously developed. Where conditions make large-scale organization desirable, some centralized direction and control is more effective. Society is thus seen as the most sophisticated piece of man's technology: it is his means of coming to terms with his environment, and it is sophisticated because it is flexible.

Although anthropology is usually thoug of as the study of primitive peoples, anthr pologists have come to reject the idea th any group can properly be thought of primitive. Moreover, anthropologists c now be found studying the peoples America, Britain, France and other a vanced societies. Dr. Jarvie shows us ho the science has grown from the study comparisons and contrasts between on society and another and how contact b tween cultures and societies has stimulate reflection on why social life is ordered t way it is, and not some other way.

Born in England in 1937, Dr. Ian C. Jarv received his Bachelor of Science degree economics and his doctorate at the Londo School of Economics. At present he is professor in the Department of Philosoph at York University, Ontario, Canada. He the author of three previous books: T Revolution in Anthropology; Hong Kong: Society in Transition; and Movies an Society.

Dr. Daniel A. Greenberg, consulting edit for the History of Science Series, receive his M.A. and Ph.D. in theoretical physi from Columbia University in 1956 ar 1960, respectively. He was on the physi faculty of Columbia University from 19. to 1963, and on the history faculty the from 1964 to 1966. Dr. Greenberg is pre ently on the staff of the Sudbury Valle School in Framingham, Massachusetts. H is the author of many articles and sever books on the history of science and physic and has also edited several history science series.